Top Secrets of

Accumulating More Money

Become Very Wealthy

Regardless of Your

Situation

D Smith

Copyright

Legal Notice

Table of Contents

Acknowledgements   V
Introduction   VI
The Death Of Jobs   1
Chapter 1: Become Your Own Boss, Own Your Destiny: 11
Chapter 2: Why You Should Want To Get Rich: The Top
Secrets Of Success   23
Chapter 3: The Three Secret Pillars Of Wealth   32
Chapter 4: The Secret Magic Formula For Uncommon
Riches   43
Chapter 5: The Safest Investment You Can Make   51
Chapter 6: How To Become A Market Wizard Like Warren
Buffet   66
Chapter 7: How To Make Money While You Sleep.   96
The Power Of Passive Income   96
Final Thoughts   139
Thank You And Let's Stay Connected   142

Acknowledgements

I would like to express my gratitude to all the people who worked hand in hand with me all throughout the entire book. I want to thank my wife, and my beautiful kids Janiah and Judah for always supporting and believing in me. And for everyone who took the time and effort to offer comments, quotes, corrections and also provide physical, emotional and mental support that assisted in making this book a reality. It would not have been possible without all your sacrifices and contributions that added to my knowledge and writing style.

Last but not least, I wish to recognize all those who worked behind the scenes and whose names have not been mentioned. I beg your forgiveness for not giving credit where it is due, but I assure you that all readers will appreciate the work put in over the years.

Introduction

So, how do you accumulate enough wealth to live a comfortable life well into retirement? This is the question we seek to answer in this book. From the onset, this book empowers to make a transition from where most people are (employed but barely surviving financially) to where you want to be rich (having enough money to live on your own terms and have the freedom to pursue your true passions).

Many of the ideas offered in other books are mere fantasies for most as these books don't deal with the financial realities of the working class and are too abstract to be of any practical benefit. That's where this book can help you, this booked is aimed at those who may not have a fortune to invest to become richer. This book was designed for people with limited financial resources.

We will look at your current financial position (whether you are in debt or have high disposable income) and from the information in this book you will be able to map out a plan for a better and more prosperous future.

Together we will look at personal finance (we have a whole two chapters dedicated to this) and form a foundation to build success. We will get to understand the basics of personal finance and wealth management. How to increase your income, the jobs and passive income opportunities you can do on a part-time basis, how to manage your expenses, the savings opportunities you have and investment options.

The book also takes you through the transition process, how do you handle the inevitable layoff or business failure and move on? Unfortunately, the cases of dismissal are now more widespread than ever. You want to know how you can transition from employment to entrepreneurship.

With this reality, we have to find alternative ways of surviving. What happens when you are laid off? What happens if your income is too little to sustain you and your family? How do you transition from employment to self-employment? These are just a few of the questions answered in this book.

We will also look at a choice you should make that has a lasting impact on your wealth.

If you are looking for ways to put your finances in order, and become financially wealthy this is the book you need. Please join me on this journey and read on.

The Death of Jobs

So let's quickly get some boring facts out of the way. The majority of people in the west earn their living via employment. This has been the best way to earn a living for hundreds of years and our entire education system is predicated upon by the need to churn out readily trained workers to replace the aging population.

However, there has been a significant shift in the world economy in the recent past. The recession continues to persist despite the confidence exuded by different governments that the job market is expanding. The number of people looking for a job continues to rise every day.

When the government releases statistics that there has been a surge in the job market, what they are not telling you is that the surge is as a result of the rise in self-employment. More people are now being pushed into self-employment, most of whom were not ready to take the leap. This is true in the U.S, Europe, Asia and all other continents. There is no doubt that there has been a shift in the job landscape.

The entrepreneurial boom witnessed today is a byproduct of the recession that many economies around the world continue to see. So, what is the trend going into the future? Is the job market Dead? That is the big question.

Rise in Unemployment and Its Implications

If you are unemployed, you may think you know all there is to know about unemployment. You know it has changed your whole family structure and security. You know what it has done to your sense of self-worth. You know the worry of where the next meal is coming from, and can you keep a roof over your family's head. You know the personal, gut-wrenching facts, but that is not all there is to know.

There is a definition of unemployment, believe it or not. It is defined as a person who does not have a job and has been looking unsuccessfully for over four weeks. There is a less personal definition. It is expressed in percentages, and it is derived by dividing the number of job seekers by the number of workers in the job force. This percentage right now is 9.3%, the highest in over a decade.

What causes unemployment, you may ask. There are several theories, one being that regulation imposed on businesses causes a decrease in the number of people hired. Some of the rules that are suspect are minimum wage laws, union activities, taxes, benefits required to be offered to employees, and any other mandatory requirements that might increase business operating expenses, thus cutting into profits.

Some economists describe a cyclic nature to unemployment, stating that such rates will rise and fall over time. That is little consolation to you if you are unemployed.

Inadequate training and education in job skills are other factors for those not being able to find employment, as is their discouragement over the outlook for work. Poverty, partly due to unemployment, is also a factor making job hunting difficult, as there aren't funds to use for the task. Mechanization decreases the number of jobs. A person's concept of how much they are worth in the job market may cause them to bypass lower- paying jobs in search of a higher-paying one.

Can we do anything to help those seeking jobs be successful? It has been suggested that incentives for businesses to encourage them to hire is a solution. Some programs might be stimulus packages, tax breaks, and programs to reward a company for expanding their business and creating jobs. For the job hunter, assistance in training for job skills will help those hardest hit by unemployment.

Some have suggested lowering the minimum wage, creating new jobs, mandating earlier retirement, job-sharing, and controlling the rate of migration would all help put more people to work. The impact of these solutions on the level of unemployment has not been adequately verified. As a consequence, not many economists or individuals have accepted them.

There are consequences of unemployment beyond economic hardship. These include an associated higher crime rate. There are more homicides and suicides linked to the unemployed people. Child abuse and alcoholism escalate. The youths are even harder hit. They cannot gain on-the-job skills and training, so their future is negatively impacted. They are often seen as employable since they have never worked and have not been able to find a job.

Family structure changes as a result of unemployment. Fathers may become the caretakers and mothers the breadwinners. The children see a change in not only the relationship between their parents but in their dealings with each family member as well. The frustrations of being unemployed may cause added discord in the household.

Even though unemployed parents have more time to spend with children, often frustration and stress make that time unproductive.

We can put a number on the economic costs, such as the decrease in the Gross Domestic Product, which is an economic health indicator. No one has been able, however, to quantify the social costs to the individual and families. Additionally, there are increased costs associated with the greater need for welfare programs, food stamps, Medicaid, and other economic programs to help those who have no job. The cost of unemployment is not just an individual thing; it is a universal one.

Lay Off: Why Unemployment is Not the End

This book will look at alternatives to becoming financially secure beyond the traditional model of employment. You may not believe that the world is heading for a depression. But even if you have no idea what the economic indicators are really saying about the future, you can still learn a great deal about how to go about adding to your net worth.

The death of jobs is real, so is unemployment. Companies are hardly hiring new employees, but in some cases, it gets so bad that some workers have to be laid off. While the economic situation may be to blame for the decline in employment, thanks to new technology. Industrial machines and robots have taken over our roles in the workplace. The robots can complete jobs hundreds of times faster than an average man and with a higher rate of efficiency.

The robots and other machines that are replacing humans in the industry lines are also cheaper to operate, do not need insurance, retirement plans, and other costs associated with maintaining employees. They work 24 hours without getting tired. With all these in mind, we must accept that the role of the human in the factories and even offices is diminishing.

Rumors have been on the air that your companies will be laying some people off. We, it is just rumors until you eventually get the letter. You are one of the victims. Are you going to be shocked by the development?

Well, there are hundreds of reasons why you think you should not be laid off. Unfortunately, your bosses think otherwise. To be safe, get out of the shock and move on. You are not the first one to be laid off, and as you will soon discover, many people are not even waiting to be laid off. People are turning in their resignation to get into self-employment. You can try getting another job, but what if it also comes with disappointments? Getting fired from our job is ground zero, it's the lowest point you can be at when trying to better yourself financially that's why we are starting here.

Here is the List of 4 Things to Do When Laid Off

#1. **Introspect**: Introspecting has nothing to do with cursing. It is all about trying to understand what triggered the layoff. Is it the change in technology that rendered your position obsolete? Is it the declining profitability that forced the company to sacrifice some employees to remain afloat? There could be many reasons, some of which may be your fault and others not. By introspecting, you get to understand the real reason why you were laid off in the first place.

#2. Relax and Rejuvenate: This sounds funny. How are you going to relax when your source of income has just been cut off? Look at it this way, in a clear state of mind; you will be able to figure out your next move. You need to relax and enjoy the free time as you flash ideas and figure out your next move.

#3. Organize and Strategize: After taking time off and relaxing, it is time to put everything together. Some people might seize the opportunity of getting laid off to launch their own business, but not all people will financially and emotionally be able to do so. If you are not ready for self-employment or business, then your next move is to find a new job.

Start by listing down the companies that might find your experience useful and then customize your resume to fit the needs of these companies. Connect and communicate with the right people in these companies. When you get a chance, prepare well for the interview. You need to have a convincing explanation why you got laid off or "moved on".

#4. Coping with Depression and Anger: The earlier you move on, the better for you. Most people waste precious time contemplating and hating the situation. In some cases, some people are unable to take it. The new job may not be coming as soon as you wish. This leads to anger and depression. In severe cases, the affected person has to be treated by a psychiatrist. You don't have to get to this point. Be positive and spend most of your energy on the next move.

The Exit Strategy When Laid Off

Is this the right time to go back to school? Yes, you need to upgrade your skills and be fresh for the new position. If you can get a new degree or a certificate, go for it. You might be facing a complete career change. Don't be afraid; it is better this way.

Well, what if you don't have the time? The solution is to work part-time while going to school. In this way, you get to cover the cost and enjoy the benefits of new skills. However, if you can afford it, you might consider staying out of work until you are through with the education. In some cases, you may take advantage of the various financial aids available.

Make use of your contacts: If you want to get a head start, just know that 80% of jobs are filled through networking. Get out and network. Make use of your contacts. There are several networking strategies, some of which are available online. Take the opportunity to make a move to your next career.

Becoming an Entrepreneur If you have been thinking about your job and have been saving for it, this is the perfect time to start. If the layoff came as a surprise, and you were not ready to get into self-employment, but you need to know that any time can be the right time. Just weigh all the pros and cons, do your research and get going. Start small and soon enough, you will make it big.

The Rise in Entrepreneurship Spirit?

There is no doubt that the recession is responsible for the death of jobs in most economies. Today, many people, including young college graduates start their entrepreneurship journey; not as a response to the urge to live out their lifelong dream, but as the means to keep a roof over their heads.

There are hundreds of examples of young individuals that go straight into self-employment after losing their jobs. It is easy to come across college graduates applying for up to a hundred jobs per week without getting any response.

The situation is worse for young adults that lose their first jobs few years into employment. There are bills to settle, and perhaps children to look after. After applying for hundreds of positions with no luck, it is only reasonable that the person considers other possible sources of income.

The business starts as a desperate measure to earn money for rent and other bills. However, in the process, you realize that the business has a potential of becoming a well-paying employer. Job security is good, but what happens when the job is not there anymore? Self-employment is the answer.

Even after setting up the business and making sure that it is running, many business founders confess that they would have preferred to be employed. Business challenges are not for the faint-hearted. There is nothing like regular income. Your earnings link directly to the effort and strategies you put in. Some months come with no income, yet the bills remain constant.

You also have no regular working hours. You work extra time, sometimes working for as much as 60 hours in a week. This does not guarantee any income. It is true for many self-employed people all over the world.

Employment is associated with job security and predictable income.

Not everybody goes into self-employment as a result of frustration, to some, it is more of a natural transition.

The Role of Changing Technology

The change in technology is the primary catalyst behind the explosion of self-employment. The Internet has completely transformed the business platform. Back in the 1980s and early 1990s, only a handful of people could afford to put resources together to start a business. It involved raising capital to buy expensive office gear. The startup capital was unimaginable.

In the past, there was no technology that could be deployed by large companies to allow their employees to work remotely. The employees had to come physically to the office from where they would interact with their colleagues.

Fast forward to today, everything has changed. You have all the technology you need to run a company on your smartphone and laptop. There is no reason to spend a fortune running a business. All you need is a little creativity and imagination, and your business is a success.

Self-employment comes with flexibility. As a skilled professional, you don't have to spend your prime years working for someone else. You can easily market your services over the internet and up your earnings to a level that your employer cannot offer you.

Companies are also finding it easier. There is no need to struggle with huge employee costs associated with maintaining employees. By outsourcing most of the services to freelancers, the companies can avoid the costs that are associated with hiring in-house workers such as the HR costs, employee benefits and bonus schemes, the pension plans and insurance costs.

The flexibility with which the skills, services, and products can be traded has given the spirit of entrepreneurship and self-employment new impetus. It works for individuals on a personal level as well as companies. This largely explains the death of job phenomenon.

Chapter 1: Become your own boss, own your destiny:

Why Self-Employment? How Do You Go About It?

For those who passed through the education system, the majority of us are pre-wired for employment. We are bred to be the worker drones in a complex system that is capitalism. Most of us as worker bees accept the life we are given. We are allowed mortgages, holidays, new cars and all the trappings of success we want. But the truth of the matter is that most worker drones end up spent and exhausted and at the end of their work lives with poor health and a poor standard of living. Some drones might be lucky enough to retire rich as their home (principle asset) may have appreciated in equity. But seldom are these fortunate few really financially free when you break things down and analyze. The majority of the workforce will only realize that the 9-2-5 model, and pension schemes are nothing but elaborate Ponzi schemes. All Ponzi schemes work because a few people are allowed to be successful, thus encouraging others to also pile into the scheme. Government debt has grown beyond what we can realistically pay back and yet people trust in a pension that is simply non-existent. Creating a business or investing is the only way you can stay ahead of the inflation curve as saving money is no longer viable with quantitative easing of the federal reserve eroding our savings.

You simply don't have a choice in the matter, you have to create more wealth than the government can erode with taxes and inflation just to keep the value of your savings.

We have been indoctrinated into thinking that jobs and pensions are safe options. The vast majority of us will tolerate the stresses of our jobs as we have no real alternative option.

This book will show you there are other options to the traditional 9-2-5. It is the purpose of this book to encourage you to get a hold of your finances and at a minimum start making a transition to self-employment. Big Business and investment are alternatives we can look at also but self-employment is the easiest transition that you can make, and can also be done while you are still working and dreaming of quitting your 9-2-5.

In reality, though, going down the path of self-employment is hard. However, many people have succeeded, and much more are succeeding. What are they doing right?

Well, all you need is a well-considered plan that is backed with realistic assumptions and well-researched facts. You also need willpower and the proper work ethics. Before you decide that this is a good time to hand over your resignation letter and dive into self-employment, there are several things you need to know.

The Positive Side of Self-Employment

Have control over your Schedule: Self-employment allows you the flexibility and the freedom to choose where to work, when to work and what to do. Your workplace can be your backyard, your garage, your living room or a rented office. Your job can begin at any time; at midnight, early in the morning or at midday.

However, you have to work out your schedule to meet your customer demands. In reality, you are likely to work for more hours than the regular 8 to 5 schedule. Your business background largely determines your schedule. You have to arrange everything depending on your priorities, and you have control over your time. It is the greatest advantage of self-employment.

Have control of what you do: As an employee, you are often "forced" to perform tasks against your will and sometimes, without you understanding the necessity of the task you are performing. In self-employment, this is different. You can clearly see the interconnection between the tasks you and your employees do and how they all connect and contribute to the overall goal of the business. Once you can define every function and how important it is, there is nothing like a boring job; after all, every task has a purpose.

You Have Control Over Profits: As a self-employed person, every task you perform and the quality of your work directly affects the profits you make. Higher sales translate to higher profits for the business owner. After settling all the pending bills and paying all employees, the profits are yours. You don't have to share the profits with shareholders.

Negative Side of Self-Employment

Irregular Income: Unlike formal employment associated with regular pay, your income in self-employment depends on your efforts and the success of the business. You make no income is you don't make sales and generate traffic within the period. Going through a month without income can be very rough.

Being in Control of Your Schedule: As much as this is a major positive attribute of self-employment, it can also be a major setback to your personal development. You have to be motivated all the time to be able to remain committed to the primary goal. Self-employment requires a lot of sacrifices, and it may not work for lazy people.

You are in control of the Business Finances: In a regular job, your employer handles several finance items like income tax, Medicare and social security. In self-employment, you have to learn to deal with such issues. You may be penalized by the IRS should you fail to keep proper records and report the tax appropriately.

Additional Implication of Self-Employment

You have a Diverse and More Challenging Work Schedule

When employed, you have the luxury to specialize and solely focus on a particular line of interrelated tasks in an appropriate department. As a self-employed person, you have responsibilities beyond your core skillset.

You have to learn and do almost everything. Even if you have employees, you have to master the tasks they perform to be able to control and approve their work.

It is a blessing but can also be a curse. You learn many things within a short period. These include different forms of marketing techniques, accounting and finance, production/manufacturing, and managing employees, and resources all at the same time.

The setback of all this is that you are more prone to making mistakes, some of which may be costly. You learn most things through mistakes.

You Have Less Protection against Failures

In regular employment, most failures are not expensive. Your employer may consider further training as the remedy to failure. However, in your own business, the success or failure of the enterprise rests solely on your shoulders. It should be motivating, but to others, it might be a burden.

Laying the Groundwork

The transition from regular employment to self-employment requires prior planning and consideration. There are several things to consider when preparing for the transition.

Efficient Utilization of Resources: Your success in self-employment is pegged on your ability to manage resources like time, money, and employees effectively. You have to organize your activities so that you have time for your family and your entertainment. You may have to make a few sacrifices, such as cutting down on TV and movie time.

Personal Production Methodology Coaching: It is often not easy to have everything done and get the results you expect. Consider enrolling in a coaching class to learn better methods of managing everything and having everything done. Most of the training are available online, in the books, audios, and videos. Such programs can be very helpful most of the time.

Have Enough Time for Sleep: Most self-employed people suffer from fatigue resulting from inadequate sleep time. Without a proper plan and schedule to handle the tasks at hand, you often get trapped trying to catch up with job-related activities. It leaves you with less time to sleep, a factor that could considerably affect your productivity, health, and motivation. You need a regular and adequate sleep pattern to be productive during the day.

Learn to be Frugal: You have to change the way you handle your finances. You need "cost versus benefit" kind of thinking. It does not mean that you have to be a tightwad, it's about being prudent. Your choices need to be based on the total cost and the value.

There are many ways in which you can practice the technique. It all starts from day-to-day decision making and develops to long term strategic decisions that will carry you throughout your business. You could find better ways to manage your bills, cut down unnecessary utility services and manage resources in a more prudent way.

Money Management Skills: You have to learn money management skills. These are the skills on how to get and retain more money than you spend over time. Self-employment means that you have to keep your financial house in order. Your credit cards need to be in order.

Learn to Save: You have to put your credit cards in order and have something to save. Get a high yielding account in which you keep every cent you have. Part of your savings will provide the capital you need once you make the move.

Communication and Networking Skills: These are core competencies that you need to work on as part of the groundwork into self-employment. These skills are essential as you need to communicate confidently and build quality connections. These are skills that you can only learn by practicing. You could also enroll in mentorship and coaching class to grasp the skills faster. Some mentorship and coaching classes are available online.

Introspection

You need to spend time pondering and answering some fundamental questions regarding your life. Introspection should point you in the right direction you ought to take. It is through introspection that you get to answer the primary questions you need to get answered before you give it a go. When setting up for self-employment, there are particular considerations:

What is your purpose in life?

This is a fundamental question that you must get right. How do you go about it? Simple, on a blank sheet of paper, write the heading, "What is My Purpose in Life?" Go ahead and write any answer that comes to your mind. Write anything, even if it is an incomplete sentence. Continue writing up to the point you write down an answer that brings tears to your eyes or a smile or a sense of peace. That is your purpose in life.

The same technique could be used to extract your core values. In a list of a hundred or more values, there are a few that will give you some inner feelings and touch your heart. These could be your core values.

After you determine your core values and purpose in life, you set your priorities in line with your goal. You are likely to be at peace with yourself when doing something closer to your purpose.

Passion Matters: When brainstorming possible business ideas, you need to figure out where your passion lies. What do you enjoy doing? To make the right judgment, you need to take a long-term view of your day to day activities. Are there particular tasks that you enjoy doing and you are comfortable doing them continuously? It could be writing, cooking, coaching, and gardening/farming or any other activity.

Are there Limitations to Your Talents? You need to know what your talents are and the limitations that could present a roadblock to your dreams. The restrictions are not always obvious; in fact, you might not have an idea of your limitations. You may need to evaluate yourself and determine your weaknesses critically. Your friends and colleagues are in a good position to help you through this process. Once you get to know your weaknesses, you need to formulate a plan to deal with these shortcomings.

Building a Plan

After you have everything (the personal habits, the mindset, and the resources) in order, the next step is to lay the groundwork for self-employment. Building the foundation before jumping into self-employment is a sure way to avoid troubles associated with the first few months of self-employment.

Brainstorming Ideas

After discovering your passion and talents, it is time to turn them into ideas that can work. The ideas should be generated from the connection between your passions and your skills. Make two separate lists; one of your talents and the second one for your passions. Try connecting the two and finding out how many ideas you can come up with that marry your passions with your talent.

If your passion is strategic board games and your talent is writing, you could connect the two and come up with several ideas. The possible ideas include blogging about strategic board games, writing articles for publication, organizing gaming events, and running a gaming shop among others.

Not everything you write down will excite you, and some may not even be realistic, let alone work. However, if your list is correct, you will quickly narrow down to an idea that works for you.

Get into Researching

As much as books, videos and audio packages about self-employment are rich sources of ideas and information relating to starting and running a business; they are never full sources of information. Be patient, take all the time you need to go through as many sources of information as possible, but customize everything to fit your personal situation. Not everything you read is true and will work; you need to employ your wisdom in choosing what is relevant and what is not.

In addition to gathering information from entrepreneurship packages, consider having a chat with a friend, relative or any person currently running a business. You are likely to gather more relevant information by sharing your thoughts and ideas with a friend in the similar business. Most people will be glad to offer information and the advice you need, all you need is to find the right person.

Develop a Sketch

Make a selection of a few ideas from the list you have brainstormed. Use the research ideas you have gathered so far to make a sketch for each of the ideas that excites you. Carefully analyze the ideas you have at hand and develop a small business plan for a few of the ideas you see the potential.

Developing a business plan helps you define the detail of each of the ideas. Some of them may sour you as you get into the details. Such ideas get dropped along the way. You continue to analyze the remaining ones at this point.

Gather More Information to Strengthen the Ideas

As you continue to eliminate the ideas that seem to sour you, the list narrows down to a few but exciting ones. You have to gather as many details as possible about the remaining ones. The sources of information remain the same, only that you are now focused and seeking accurate information. This step should take you closer to understanding the most viable business idea that is practical and appealing to you.

Executing the Plan

By now, everything should be ready. You have a clear agenda. Your life is in order. Your habits are set to run a business. The time has come when you have to take the first step. All you are now waiting is to hand over the resignation letter and bid goodbye to your colleagues. So, how do you progress?

Use free time to cultivate your business

If you can start the business in your free time, it is best to get it started before you resign. The business should be running and start generating sales. Keep investing your free time, effort and financial resources to maintain the business.

Define the Business Success Benchmarks

As you begin the business, you need to have a clear agenda. Set the business success thresholds. Don't go for the bare minimums; you need better than average. Are the inflows and profits good enough to sustain you without the salary you are used to? Your source of income is going to be your business. The business should, therefore, generate enough to sustain you and still save to finance growth and expansion of the business.

It is through these benchmarks that you will be able to decide whether it is time to resign or not. Once the business starts running, it becomes more demanding. It is easy to gauge if it is the right time to quit or not.

Leverage Your Current Employment with Your New Business

It is through the initial successes in your business that you will develop the courage to hand over your resignation letter. However, you don't have to be rude or burn bridges. Take advantage of your position in the current workplace to build connections and contacts that can be helpful in your business.

A smooth transition plan works for you in two main ways. First, it is a big boost to your business. The contacts you make and network are valuable assets to the business. The second benefit is to you as an individual. By exiting in a friendly fashion, your employers will not refuse to open doors should you ask for an opportunity to return.

Make the Move

The time comes when you have to walk the talk. When everything falls into place, hand in your resignation letter and move to your business after the notice period has elapsed. In this way, you can focus all your effort on the business and grow it to its full potential.

Chapter 2: Why You Should Want to Get Rich: The Top Secrets of Success

Many people want to get rich. For them the question, 'why get rich' is a ridiculous one. They feel like the objective of getting rich is just a natural part of living. There are some for whom the answer to the question is not so clear. Either they think that others who seek to get rich site selfish, petty reasons, or that it is unnecessary to get rich to live a good, decent life.

Our attitudes towards wealth are shaped by our nuclear family, religious upbringing, society and immediate environment or social circles.

The truth is money is neutral energy. Money is neither good or bad, it simply makes the good even better and the bad even worse. Money will not solve your problems, take it from me. Don't waste your life trying to get money because you think it will solve your problems because it won't.

This book is not about getting rich so you can have all the material possessions you see celebrities on reality shows have. This book is geared towards the 'worker drones' the dads and moms that grind away day after day just to make ends meet. This book is about creating the quality of life that hard working people deserve but governments are trying ever so hard to ensure they will not have, through money mastery.

It is important for those who want to get rich that they clearly define the reasons why they want to get rich. They cannot say that they want it 'just because.' They should not want it for the wrong reasons. The truth is that most people are often afraid of wealth for the simple reason that they are afraid of change.

Change scares people as money presents a whole new set of problems than being broke does, so sub-consciously we may wish to remain broke as there is safety in what we know.

But the only real constant is life, is change. In life we will always have problems, that's a given and money will not in any way eradicate this but here are a few reasons to get rich.

1. Quit job and find fulfillment in your passions
2. Travel and experience the world (take time to live in various countries to absorb the culture)
3. Pay off debts
4. Give to charities and causes you believe in
5. Invest in the disenfranchised communities (Ghettos)
6. Create scholarship programs for smart poor children
7. Take care of your elderly parents
8. Provide Medicare assistance for friends and family
9. Financial legacy to ensure children are educated and futures are secure
10. Build your own space rocket (just kidding ☺)

But you get the picture, the list is endless as to the possibilities of what you could do with money if you look outside yourself.

Secrets of Getting Rich

Anybody can be rich; you don't need any special talent. You don't have to be born with a silver spoon or born with the luck of the Irish. In reality, the majority of self-made millionaires are ordinary people. It is their habits that set them apart from the rest of us.

Becoming rich is all about changing your habits. There are decisions that you must make and specific skills you must acquire but anyone can do it. In fact, becoming rich is Below are a few ways people become rich:

a) Get to Work Earlier

b) Grow your disposable income

c) Practice financial skills

d) Learn to save and invest wisely

Certainly, there are hundreds of ideas on how you can get rich. However, all these revolve around working smart, practicing financial skills (putting into practice the principles of financial education), learning to save and investing wisely to earn extra income.

Secret #1: Report to work an hour early

This book is designed to be a pragmatic approach to money mastery. So we will start with a simple principle those of you still in a 9-2-5 job can put into practice immediately. Those who are already working for themselves may also put this to practice and see results.

Many dream of becoming finally secure but few of us think about a detailed plan of how exactly we are going to achieve it.

Having a positive attitude is not enough if you want to be successful. Visualization will not "attract" anything to your life if you are not willing to work hard and take action.

It is rare in this day and age with the proliferation of information that we can have an information advantage over competitors for long. To become an entrepreneur, you need to have an edge. Visualization and having great information is fine but chances are there are thousands with the same dream and information.

What will set you apart from others is action. I was in a third world country and noticed there wasn't a decent coffee shop anywhere. I remember telling my good friend out there the he would make a fortune if he opened one.

Like the typical worker drone he proceeded to tell me the reasons why a coffee shop wouldn't work in his country. I went back to see him years later, and there were major coffee franchises all over the place and my friend although had aspirations of success and the information needed to succeed he did nothing and was still trapped in the monotonous routine of his 9-2-5 grind.

Getting rich requires that you have the edge over everybody else in virtually everything you do. One productivity tip entrepreneurs or CEO's use is waking up early and reporting to work earlier. This gives you the advantage over the rest of the pack.

It means that you can work and polish on a few things before the rest of your colleagues' report to the office. This allows you to make additional contacts, learn some essential skills, and polish your reports. An hour extra a day seems like nothing but it amounts to over 250 hrs. a year. There is simply no way anyone at work will be able to compete with you. This can also be applied to business, in getting an advantage over competitors.

Most people who make it rich in life are early risers. It is the unwritten rule of success. If you want to get rich, you need to have life goals. These are the lifetime achievements. However, the life goals must be broken down to five-year goals, one-year goals, one-month goals and then to one-day goals. With this kind of focus, you get a sense of direction. Everything you do must be well thought of and in line with your goals.

You have to learn something helpful every day, remember something, and do something that contributes to your goals.

You need to learn the habits that can make you prosperous and progress in life. The next step is to practice what you learn and get to enjoy your successes.

The secret is to do something extra than what you are doing today. However, to achieve this, you will have to get up earlier than usual. With this, you get a chance to plan your day properly and do something extra. It is the extra things that you do that translates to an additional thousands or millions and increased wealth.

Secret #2: Grow your disposable income

You don't necessarily need to earn millions to become rich, but your income should be more than average. It should be able to cater for your day-to-day needs and you should still be able to save and invest after all the bills are paid. If you learn the pillars of wealth you can become rich with virtually any income. The only major difference is that it may take longer, for those on low-income jobs (< $40,000).

Disposable income is the catalyst with which you will build your portfolio of assets and investments. The quickest way for many is to get a higher paying job.

Better paying job

Many have grown disillusioned by their jobs and quit too soon for a life of entrepreneurship. But if you can start a part-time business on the side while at work, then why not change jobs and get a better paying job, so you have more to invest. Here are a few tips to getting more income at your job.

1. Ask for a rise
2. Apply for a new job
3. Seek a promotion
4. Upskill and become more valuable
5. Work overtime

Spend Less

There are many other methods and hopefully we will go over these later, but an often overlooked way to grow disposable income is getting a grip with spending. I remember when I was struggling starting up some of my businesses, while still in a 9-2-5. To my horror when I looked how I was spending my monthly pay check from my job I realized that 9% was spent on entertainment, 15% was spent on eating out whilst at work. All it took was for me to downgrade my satellite tv package and take packed lunches to work and I was able to free up 20% of my salary that was being wasted and I funneled that into my side hustles. Take stock of what you are spending your money on. You won't die if you cancel your Netflicks, Cable TV, Gym membership and other comforts we pay for that we can temporary do without as we sacrifice to become financially independent.

Other methods

1. Real estate
2. Stocks
3. Bonds
4. Options
5. E-commerce
6. Freelancing

As we will be having a more detailed look for now we will not look at the others. But the general idea is that you should look for ways to bring in more money on a monthly basis.

Secret #3: Practice financially valuable skills

The financially valuable skills are the skills that contribute to business profitability and wealth management. Not all skills are economically valuable skills, but the art of earning more all the time requires the financially valuable skills. The next chapter discusses the financial skills through the three pillars of wealth management.

Secret #4: Invest in a side business

If your income is sufficient to cater for the basic needs, our next objective is to save and invest. However, it's only possible to save and invest if you understand and practice the discipline of money management.

The sure way to get rich is through investment. Consequently, it is a good idea to invest in a side business. In this way, you get to earn a higher-than-average income at the end of the month.

Although you can opt to quit your job and concentrate on your business, this should only be done once you are ready, and everything is in place as described in the next chapter. It will also be crazy to mortgage your house and jump into a business that is not ready. The idea is to be ready when the time comes to get involved in business fully.

Your best bet is in the so-called **"chicken entrepreneurship."** This is the concept of entrepreneurship in which the entrepreneur starts off slowly and gets to learn the nitty-gritty of the side business while still enjoying the steady income from the primary job.

Side businesses should not take your attention from the primary job. It is something that you love and should be able to manage on weekends or evenings without compromising your primary job. This should be the case even if you own and maintain the primary job.

Today, there are hundreds of possible ideas for side businesses. These range from consultancy, freelance writing, and real estate to investment in the securities market. Some of these ideas are discussed in the latter chapters.

Secret #5: Invest the rest safely

The Secrets #1, #2, and #3 should leave you with enough income to invest in the side business and retain something to save and invest. The security and safety of your hard-earned money should be your primary concern. However, beyond that, you must also consider the return you are earning.

The return on investment (ROI) and risk factors should be the guide when seeking for good yields. The difference between the return of 2% and the return of 22% can mean the difference between $100,000 and $10 million at the point of retirement.

There are several opportunities in stocks, bonds, real estate investment opportunities and several other securities.

Chapter 3: The Three Secret Pillars of Wealth

We often view the rich and wealthy as lucky. We often say that if we went to the same schools as they did, or had the same parents we would have turned out just as wealthy. But this is not the case as much as we would like to think that millionaires are lucky or dishonest, the simple truth is they do not possess any esoteric qualities.

There are people who went to Harvard and make five to six figures a year, but there are also people who barely graduated high school and make five to six figures a year. There are millionaires who went to Oxford university in England and there are millionaires who grew up in drug-infested housing projects.

Studies of billionaires showed that educational background and net worth of parents rarely made a difference. There is also no commonality in terms of religious beliefs, gender, politics, sexual orientation or age. The one common attribute amongst the mega-wealthy is their mindset.

Millionaires have a money belief system that fuels their ambition. Millionaires understand money and know how to use it to create wealth. I once knew of two brothers who were given the same opportunities to succeed in life. One did well but the other became a multi-millionaire. I once asked the multi-millionaire brother what do you think is the major difference in why you were able to excel? He replied "we are the same in our education, opportunities and belief.... But what sets me apart is not how I think......it's what I do consistently"

While allot of people find the new age "law of attraction appealing", it's only when thoughts become actions and actions become habits that financial change will come.

If your objective is to be rich, you have to develop habits that will support your objectives. The next task after building the right habits is committing to the habits. It is not often easy to practice wealth management skills, but you have to commit to the habits to succeed in accumulating wealth.

When we talk of commitment, we are referring to the effort and sacrifice you are willing to put in. Commitment once meant an irreversible decision. Commitment means that once my mind is made up and I have made a decision then I will not let anything persuade me otherwise.

This is one of the most endearing habits of millionaires, they are committed to the process of becoming millionaires. At some point in their lives, it could be at campus at Harvard, or on the basketball courts or a ghetto, a decision is made, that becomes irreversible in the mind of the would-be millionaire. That's why millionaires can face more discouragement and setbacks than the average person. They are committed to one-day succeeding and they refuse to be deterred by failure. They do not give up until they make it, they are committed.

Take a look at any weight loss program; it involves adopting a new way of life. The lifestyle changes include a commitment to a healthy diet and eating habit and regular exercising. The success of any diet is determined by how committed you were to the diet. So the question is how committed are you to your life? How committed are you to success?

In order to change your finances, you need to be committed to the process of transformation. Changing habits is not as easy as it sounds. It involves developing new plans for each day. The plan must be in line with your short-term, medium-term and long-term goals. The new plans also touch all the realms of life. For instance, you will change what, how and where you shop, where you live, what and how you eat and even your friends and people you interact with.

Before discussing the three pillars of wealth, it is important to understand what wealth is. Most people think wealth is money; some define wealth as purchasing power. In reality, though, wealth is abundance. If you can live financially free with no worry, consider yourself wealthy.

To determine if you are wealthy draw up a list of assets and liabilities. If you are still in employment, draw up two asset/liability lists. One which includes your income from your job and the other that doesn't. If you remove your income from your job and can't survive then you are not rich regardless of how many zeros on your paycheck ☺.

When you commit to building wealth, you are essentially committing to transforming your lifestyle with the three pillars of wealth management; debt, income, and investment.

Pillar One – Income

Income and wealth are two different and distinct things. Having a high-income job does not guarantee wealth. Look at lawyers and doctors, they have a good income, and are likely to be labeled as wealthy. However, are they really wealthy?

A top notch athlete is a good example. The headlines of athletes signing billion-dollar endorsements are so familiar. However, soon after retirement, these athletes are back in the headlines, this time for the wrong reasons. They are applying for bankruptcy. As much as they have been enjoying high income, they failed to practice the second and third pillars of wealth.

For most people income is just a way to keep a roof over your head and food on the table. The majority have nothing left to invest after taking care of the basics. Sooner or later, people on payroll get tempted to use credit cards. The banks and financial institutions are more than ready to offer credit facilities.

It is not in the banks best interest to offer you sound unbiased advice. Bank financial advisers are driven by sales targets and not the need to offer you sound financial advice.

All advice offered by the banks is geared at them making money and nothing else. So, the responsibility for sound financial decision lies solely in your court. Before you think of asking for investment advice, you must get a grip of your debt and raise your income.

Your goal from this point on is to add assets to your portfolio but also to grow your income. Before you spend your next dollar think about if you really, really need to spend that dollar.

The more income you generate the more you will have to pay off debts and to invest. Income is typically generated from the assets you possess. If you have a string of rental properties then you have an asset in the property, liability in the mortgage and income and cashflow in the rent collected every month.

As explained earlier you have a finite amount of time you can offer for money, hence working a 9-2-5 is not a particularly great way to leverage your time and your life (your principle asset). With a little bit of ingenuity, you can create a business that becomes your principle bread earner and can be scaled up when you want to generate more income. With a business, you can hire more people, offer more services, launch new products or even raise your prices to generate more money.

But with a job you are limited in the income you can generate. To become a master of money, you will have to become a master of income, and learn how to grow your income independently of your job.

Pillar Two – Expenses

Building wealth is not solely dependent on the level of income you earn. To build lasting wealth you will have to learn to control your expenses. It is more to do with living within your means. Depending on your level of income, you need to settle on a reasonable and comfortable lifestyle that allows you to save something for the future.

Most people get possessed with the material wealth. In the actual sense, no one cares about where you live, what car you drive and what you eat every day. If you have no control over your spending, you have at most just a tiny chance of building lasting wealth.

Several people continue to maintain an extravagant lifestyle long after retirement. What might surprise you is that most of these people never actually made a huge income during their career life. These people were able to control their expenses, accumulate significant wealth over time and get enough to last them through retirement.

In the contrast, we come across high-income families burdened with debts. It is not wise to get indebted if you are thinking of success in the long-term.

Debt Management

Debt refers to a leveraged financial position. It is the acquisition of financial resource based on a contractual obligation to pay back within the allotted time period under the agreed terms (interest, insurance, default consequences etc.).

Debt can be both secured and unsecured. Secured debt means there is some type of assets that is put up as collateral for the loan, while with unsecured loans there is usually no asset involved.

Mortgages can be described as secured loans as the bank technically owns the house until you fully fulfill your obligation. One of the most powerful secrets of financial prosperity is leverage. Leverage is simply OPM (other people's money). OPM is the quickest way to accelerate both poverty and prosperity.

Debt is normal and is necessary for financing the operation of most companies, organizations, and government. At the individual level, debt offers a solution to acquiring assets easily, financing purchases and providing for other needs.

Debt however is a ticking time bomb. When used wisely it can really explode your wealth rapidly. If debt is not managed properly and you get into debt for frivolous reasons, then it's only a matter of time before destruction (or the bailiffs) come knocking at the door.

We all attest to the fact that it is often appealing to acquire something today with the promise of paying for it in the future. Purchasing the item is associated with pleasure, and we often desire to enjoy the pleasure now.

The easy credit of the modern era has fueled our consumer based economies and turned the working class into credit junkies. Debt is up there with inflation and taxes as the top hindrance to people having the ability to save and invest.

Many addicts if not careful, will end up borrowing from person A to pay person B, and from person C to pay person A, and the vicious cycle continues.

It is a negative spending habit that you must drop if you want to be wealthy one day. Instead of focusing on the pleasure you are going to derive from the temporal gratification of the short-term, to become a money master you must think of the long and medium term impact on your finances. When you take out $10,000 from a bank to visit Bora Bora on your dream vacation, financed at 15% APR for 5 years, what impact does that have on your financial security? What if you were to use the money instead for the down payment on some rental real estate?

In the first scenario you will have the time of your life for a few weeks but spend years paying this debt off and hinder your future prospects. In the second scenario, you create and asset that pays back the loan for itself with the potential of an increase in equity value for the underlying assets. How many trips to Bora Bora could you afford if you create a business that flourishes?

Previously I mentioned two brothers that had equal opportunities but varying success. Let's look at an example at how they view debt.

Scenario 1: Brother A (Worker drone) wants a new car so he gets a loan from the bank and supplements it with his savings to get a brand new (at the time) 2013 Porsche Panamera. He feels good about himself as his car is a real head-turner and status symbol. In 5 years he pays 130% of the nominal value of the car back to the bank and trades it in second hand at 40% of its value when new. Losing in real terms the money spent on the car.

Scenario 2: Brother B also wanted a new car and his case he decided he wanted a Bentley continental GT. So, he goes to the bank to get a loan 3 times as much as his brother got for his Porsche. But instead of going to the nearest dealer and putting in an order for his Bentley, he brought a small fleet of nearly new saloons, fitted them with the Uber App and got drivers to agree to a profit share system. After 5 years the loan is virtually paid off and he now has enough money coming from his taxi business to buy 3 Bentleys a year in cash if he wanted to. But the truth is he still drives the same old beat-up car he always has. This brother understands opportunity cost and would rather keep expanding his portfolio of assets than buy luxury goods. This is the essential difference in mindset in how the poor and rich regard debt. The poor use it for temporal gratification even though they are losing long-term, while the rich are happy to suffer short-term for long-term gain.

Debt used to elevate income is a good debt; debt used for consumptions and other pleasures is a bad debt that you need to avoid.

Pillar Three – Investments

Investment is the process of managing our positive cashflow of excess/accumulated wealth to earn extra income. To become a master of money you must learn to invest wisely. Here are a couple of things I think would be highly helpful for newbies looking to start this journey.

1. Join a real estate seminar (often free initially before up-sell to advanced seminar)
2. Read books on stock market and start watching financial news channels and research everything you don't understand
3. Read the Financial times or other financial publications
4. Watch YouTube videos that introduce the various types of investment.
5. Learn to read company financial reports

Before you invest a single penny, you should know that the investment world (especially stocks) is very competitive and you will be up against seasoned veterans who have more tools and experience at their disposal.

Many naively think they will develop more skill in a year than the seasoned traders have in twenty years. This is the foolish way to approach investing. Those with a high level of money mastery proficiency seek the safer long-term options and transition slowly into medium or short-term plays as they acquire more skill over the years or as opportunity presents itself.

It is not often easy to get the nest-egg to build up and bring you extra income. Investment is an art; it takes years to learn.

Investment habits can be learned but you need to be patient as being over-zealous and rushing in will only lead to you losing everything. You can acquire investment skill with time so be cautious. The real trick to investment is not in learning to make 10 X returns in your trades but it's the ability not to lose your nest egg. Portfolio management is one of the most important skills you need to learn and is rated even higher than the ability to pick winning stocks by the best traders in the world. Learn to cut losses and maximize profits when they present themselves.

So, is saving the same as investment? No, saving and investment is different. Saving is all about getting aside cash for future use and attempting to earn as much interest as possible to beat inflation. If you don't go beyond savings, you soon have nothing left after the savings is spent.

In the contrast, investments are not spent. You only spend part of the return, but the investment continues. The only time you should think of selling the investment is for a strategic reason. Should you sell the investment, invest money into another investment with better returns?

The portion you spend should be the returns such as rental income, interest from fixed income assets, or dividends from stocks.

However, it is not often easy to get to a point where we only spend the returns and leave the principal intact. The reasons may vary, but the primary cause of this is the lifestyle you adopt soon after you acquire extra income. It is human nature to want more than what we currently own. At the time of retirement, you are likely to spend part of the principal to sustain your lifestyle.

The three pillars that underpin wealth are income, debt management (leveraging debt) and investment. To be considered a true money master, you must master all 3. You must grow your income starting now, you must manage your debt better and use debt wisely and once you gave mastered pillars 1 and 2 you must invest the newly found positive cashflow wisely.

Chapter 4: The secret magic formula for uncommon riches

The power of compound interest

One of the common platitudes I hear all the time is "don't work harder work smarter" while I agree we must work smarter to gain an edge, to be successful in any endeavour you cannot afford to stop working hard as if you do, you open the door to a competitor that has the same information you have but is willing to work harder and longer than you are. I often say to people always assume your competition has the same information you do, always assume he is smarter than you, and strive to outsmart and outwork him.

But as stated previously you only have a finite amount of time a resource. So working smart is not about having more information and being intelligent as it's impossible to always stay in front as others will always innovate just to get in front of you or to at least catch-up. Working smart is about learning how to leverage resource (not just information). One of the resources you can leverage and get to work harder for you is your money.

I was once chastised by my mentor who told me "the problem with your generation is, you are busy but not productive, and your money is lazy." I must admit at the time I only partially understood what he was saying.

The truth of the matter is nobody will tolerate an employee who spends their entire day on Facebook and barely even does 25% of their work hours if that, such an employee will most likely get fired, because they are lazy. But we also have lazy money. What is lazy money? It's money that sits in the bank all day and does absolutely nothing. Lazy money is good at faking; my mentor would say. It pretends to be appreciating in value, but when you factor inflation over a long time span you realize that lazy money loses value.

On the other hand, there is money that never sleeps and rests. This is the sort of money you want my mentor would say. Your money should only stay at a bank temporally as it awaits deployment into another venture. By making your money work hard you activate the secret law of wealth called compound interest.

What is compounding Interest?

We are most familiar with interest that accrues from debt. We have to pay interest on the money we borrow. However, it is not always so; the interest can be made to work in your favor, and not against you. It enables you to enjoy interest on the money you are saving and investments.

In its simplest form, Compound interest is the interest calculated on the initial principal plus the interest calculated on the accumulated interest in the preceding periods. It simply means that you are earning interest on interest. What better way to grow wealth rapidly?

In the case of simple interest, the interest is calculated on the principal only. The compound interest, therefore, leaves you much richer than simple interest. It allows you to earn extra money from the interest you earn in addition to the interest from the initial investment. The wealth grows rapidly, and you have your money working for you.

The power of compounding

You have all reasons to start saving now; it is the only sure way to your financial success. You have to save even if you think all you have is a paltry sum. In reality, starting early is more important than the initial capital when you are just starting.

Did you know that procrastination is the true assassin of opportunities? If you have not heard of this phrase, now you have. This is a phrase that you will come across quite often when reading inspirational books related to wealth, getting rich and investing.

Every year you put off saving and investing, you make your retirement goals harder to realize.

On the surface, compounding interest is innocuous and boring. "My money is earning less than 3 percent in a savings account, is it even reasonable that there is enough interest that can start earning interest?" This is a familiar question? What if you have it saved in a mutual fund where it earns 8 percent?

In reality, in the short term, there is not much difference in 8% interest rate in a mutual fund and 3% interest in a high-yield savings account unless we are talking about huge sums of money.

In the long-term however, the difference is as clear as day and night. In the course of 10, 20 or 30 years, there will be a significant difference in the balances of each of the accounts. Your investment goals should be oriented to the long-term goals rather than the short-term goals.

Money masters look at short-term plans but also plan for 20-30 years in the future. I have met 40-year-olds that are struggling now and 40-year-olds who worked 3 jobs when they were 20 so they could invest in property. Which of the 40-year-olds do you think are now mega rich?

But sadly not all the 40-year-olds have learned their lesson. While the rich are planning another 20-30 years the working class just put their heads in the sands in the hope that their pension or current homes will save them somehow.

Saving Is the Key to Wealth

If you are not yet aware of it, the point is that you have to spend less than you earn, and save the difference. This is the theme running on this book from the first chapter to the last one. You are not going to get rich if you are spending all your income and borrowing (getting into debt) to make up the difference.

The society is full of people who want to live a life that is not within their means. Banks and other financial institutions are always more than willing to give them a credit facility and push them deeper into trouble.

The rich friends, neighbors, and colleagues are not rich because they earn more than you do, they are rich because they save and invest more than you do.

You may be skeptical now, but as you read more books on wealth building and wealth management, you will get convinced that this is the reality. The motivational book titled, "The Millionaire Next Door" by Stanley and Danko, it is so clear that is it not high income that leads to wealth but saving. Let's be clear, high income does not hurt, if anything, high income is what you need to save more within a shorter time.

You become wealthy only by spending less than what you earn, saving the extra, accumulating to capital that you can then invest to earn more. It is a cycle.

It is clear that saving is your key to wealth, but what is the hand that turns that key to unlock the door called wealth? If you guessed time, you guessed right. You need time to unlock this door.

If you can increase your income from side businesses, a job with more salary package or investment, then do, because this allows you to save more, and get wealthier faster.

How Does Compounding Interest Work?

Imagine that you invest something in a mutual fund and leave it untouched for a period of time; in one decade your investment will grow significantly if all you do is just reinvest the income or dividends generated. The point is demonstrated in the example below.

Take an example of three people; Jack, Jane and John, who are all born in the same year. They all save in an account with annual interest pegged at 7%, but there is a difference in when they start saving and the frequency at which they make savings.

Jack invests $5,000 every year from the time he is 18. He stops when he hits 28. Jack has invested a total sum of $50,000 in 10 years (principal amount).

Jane also invests the same amount of $5,000 every year, but she begins at the age of 28; that is the same year Jack stopped. She invests $5,000 every year until she retires at the age of 58. She will have invested a total of $150,000 in a matter of 30 years.

John on the other hands saves the same amount ($5,000) every year but begins at the age of 18 and continues until the retirement age of 58. He will have to save a total of $200,000 in 40 years.

At the end of 58 years, this is the balance in their accounts:

	Principal	**Balance**
Jack	$50,000	$602,070
Jane	$150,000	$540,741
John	$200,000	$1,142,811

Jane invested 3-times amount Jack invested, but Jack has more in his account than Jane. Jack saved for only ten years while Jane saved for 30 years. Why the difference?

Well, that is the power of compounding interest. In the ten years that Jack saved, he earned an investment return that continued to snowball for the rest of 30 years. The snowballing effect is so drastic that a late saver like Jane cannot catch up. This would be the case even if Jane saved for 20 years more than Jack. Jack had the advantage of time, and there is no way Jane was going to catch up with him unless to increase the principal she was going to save each year.

Take a look at John's balance. He is the most diligent saver of the three. He begins saving early (at 18) and never stops until retirement (at 58). He ends up with an amount that is significantly higher than either Jack or Jane.

This examples shows what can happen if you start early and consistently save until retirement. This example assumes and interest rate of 7% (which as of 2016 is unlike due to records low-interest rates).

How to get rich slowly

So, what can you do to make compound interest work for you? Here are the tricks.

1. **Start Early**: As demonstrated in the example, it is important to start early for compounding to work in your favor. The best way to start early is to start today and not tomorrow.

2. **Save Regularly**: Make saving your priority. You have to be disciplined and make sure you save every month. Exploit all opportunities you have to maximize your contributions.

3. **Patience Pays**: Don't get tempted to withdraw part of your savings or investment. The only way to have compounding work for you is by allowing your golden egg nest to grow. To enjoy the magic of compounding interest, you have to be patient until the end. Compounding creates a snowball of money. It begins with small returns at the beginning, but as

the time continues, the returns get bigger and bigger.

Chapter 5: The safest investment you can make

Investing in Real Estate

Investment in real estate has been in existence for as long as human civilization. It is one of the oldest forms of investment, and the returns never disappoint. Today, any serious investor has real estate in his portfolio. It comes with constant, but unique cash flows, profitability, liquidity that regularly outperform the other classes of investment.

Its net worth characteristics and the diversification benefits give it an edge over several other investment opportunities.

This chapter offers the introductory concepts required for investing in real estate. This chapter also takes readers through an in-depth analysis of the concepts, investors require before getting into each class of investment.

Seasoned investors may know all the concepts that we will discuss in this chapter but chances are even the seasoned of investor could learn something new.

Knowledge is power so equip yourself by studying real estate. Many think that because they flipped their family home once or twice they are now property experts. But as seasoned pro's will tell you anybody can make money during a bubble. But could you still make money with real estate, during a recession?

What Is Real Estate Investment?

Real estate investment is a set of activities including operating, investing and financing the activities that are all centered on making money from physical/tangible properties and or cash flows that are tied to physical properties. With this definition, it is clear that real estate investment can be narrowed down to several types. As an investor, there are myriad of classes to choose from when considering investing. You can create a portfolio out of different types of real estate.

Investing in Real Estate for Income Generation

In its simplest and purest form, the basic idea that determines real estate investment decision is the need to earn income. The investor who acquires a piece of tangible property is known as a landlord.

The property could be a raw farmland with crops or an empty land in a prime location in an urban center. It could also refer to an empty land in any part of the country or a land with office buildings. The land with industrial warehouse, rental houses or even natural features like a quarry, mineral deposits, privately owned lakes, forests, mountains, or game reserves, it does not matter, all these qualify as a real estate investment.

The role of the landlord is to locate a person who has the need to use the property without owning it. This person is known as the tenant. The landlord and the tenant come to an agreement in which the tenant is allowed to get access to the real estate, use it under specific terms, within a period of time and with some limitations.

The restrictions and agreement are guided by the laws laid out in Federal, state and local laws. These laws govern the terms that inform the lease contract and the rental agreement.

In exchange for accessing and using the property as agreed, the tenant pays an agreed sum of money. The payment that the tenant makes to the landlord is known as the rent. The owner earns regular rental income from this agreement.

For many investors, investing in real estate is more predictable and comes with more psychological advantages as compared to other forms of investments including investment in stocks and bonds.

Psychologically, an investor feels good when they drive by the property, take a look, touch it with their hands and relax as they supervise repair works. The investor can choose what color to use when painting, what design from an architect to choose when building rentals, shopping malls, office blocks or industrial warehouse on the property.

The investor can also use his negotiation skills as the landlord to bargain on the amount of rental income to be paid by the tenant. The psychological effect of owning a piece of real estate is significantly different from holding papers that give you the right to stocks and bonds.

However, even real estate investors are likely to get misguided from time to time, just like the stock investors during the period of the stock market bubble during which they insist that capitalization rate does not matter. Don't fall for this lie.

As long as your rental rates are priced correctly, there is nothing that can stop you from enjoying a satisfactory rate of return after having accounted for the rate of the property, the property income taxes, the insurance and a reasonable depreciation reserve and any other expenditure including security and repairs.

Time is the most valuable asset you are ever going to own in your life. If you measure the option of investing in real estate in comparison to investing in other classes of investment in terms of time, you quickly agree that there is nothing as valuable to investors as passive income. Real estate investment is an opportunity for passive investment.

With real estate, you can hire management services to take care of your property. The property management company takes charge of the management and handles day to day management activities in exchange for a small percentage of the rental income. It allows you to earn income from the property with no active involvement. You have steady cash flows of income with all the time to enjoy your income.

However, you must also understand that as time goes by, competition in the real estate industry will become harder and harder. The more investors venture into property investing, the more difficult it is becoming to compete in this real estate business (especially for the novice investors). Years ago there wasn't that much competition at real estate auctions. It was easier to find a fixer-upper and make a good profit. These days the prices at auctions have gone up due to as the influx of novices who speculate higher than they should in a desperate bid to acquire property. The influx of new investors and effective marketing tactics by savvy investors makes it difficult as a whole for everyone. In this day and age, you really need to know what you are doing as the margin for failure is much smaller. Gone are the days when you get a property for nothing miscalculate on renovation costs and still make huge profits.

The real estate market has shown signs of resilience even in the midst of a worldwide recession, a fact that has influenced many investors to consider this class of investment. Even though things appear to be saturated, if you are willing to work hard you can still make a killing.

You must first understand the industry thoroughly. Investors should know the ins and outs, the pros and cons of the business. In other words, know about the business thoroughly, so I can't emphasize highly enough the importance of investment education.

Once you understand the ins and outs of real estate from a technical perspective, you then need to work on the next most vital attribute you need to have, networking skills.

Having an extensive network is non-negotiable in real estate. Through your network you can get privileged information on real estate before it's even made public and goes on the market. Having a good network and great reputation as a business person will set you head and shoulders above the rest.

There are two practical ways to make money in property investing. One is by renting, and another one is by buying and selling. In both ways, you will undoubtedly increase your earnings substantially. Armed with the right marketing strategies, investing in properties will surely give you a very fruitful life. Property investing is a safe way in invest your money if done carefully.

Types of Real Estate Investments Available for You

Beyond renting and buying and selling properties, there are other forms of real estate investment. Property investment can be broken down into different classes, each with unique benefits and drawbacks.

Each class also comes with various brokerage practices, rent cycles, and economic characteristics. These include:

- Rental real estate

- Commercial real estate

- Retail real estate

- Industrial real estate

- Mixed-Use real estate

You can get involved in any of the above categories in a number of ways. There are three major players in real estate. The bank, the mortgagee and the tenant (if property is rental property). The only two players that make money are the bank and the investor or mortgagee. The tenant is at the bottom of the pyramid and is the one who works a 9-2-5 in order to pay-off the landlord's mortgage ☺.

You can become a banker by financing real estate deals at favorable terms. The banker and tenant have the least risk. The banker technically owns the house until it is paid for. Over 25 years the banker makes a fortune in interest rate repayments. By underwriting private mortgages for companies and individuals, you enjoy return from a higher interest that compensates for the additional risk. You could even have a lease-to-own credit provision in such arrangements.

The other alternative is to invest in mezzanine securities. This allows you to lend money to an investor for a real estate project. This debt can, later on, be converted into equity ownership if the investor fails to repay. This form of investment is common in developing hotel franchises.

The sub-specialties in real estate investments:

Leasing a space and then renting it out: This involves tying part of your capital in a property by entering into a long-term contract in which you rent a bigger room, subdivide the space and carry out modifications before sub-leasing the same space to tenants at a higher rate. Take an example of a big business block in the city; the mobile workers can buy office time from larger tenants in the property.

Acquiring tax-lien certificates: These are considered to be esoteric forms of real estate investment. They are not very appropriate, especially in the case where the investor is inexperienced. However, under the right circumstances, with the right person at the right time, this form of investment can generate high returns enough to compensate for all the effort and the risks involved.

Home ownership: This is the typical real estate investment that you are most likely familiar with. This is probably the safest bet as you will always need somewhere to live. But you are investing in a home and it's your primary asset, then you will need to evaluate if your home is in a location with great potential or are you living where you're living because its 5 mins away from grandma. If you are investing in home ownership, you need to treat more like a business and less like an expensive convenience.

Real Estate Investment and Tax Benefits

There are several reasons to start investing in properties as already discussed. There are reasons like stability, leverage, capital gains, and constant cash flows among others. These are all good reasons but have you considered the tax benefits of investing in real estate.

There is no bigger expense you are going to incur in your life like tax expense. So, how does real estate help you reduce your taxes? There are several tax reliefs you can enjoy by investing in the real estate business such as depreciation, equity, deductible expenses and tax credit.

Depreciation

The government policy favors individuals to go into real estate and owned properties. The investors are therefore given several incentives, one of which is depreciation. In reality, the property value will likely go "UP" over a period of time. Even with this fact, investors are allowed to report a "loss" in the property value every year.

Take an example of a residential property. The property's lifetime is estimated at 27.5 years. If you sell your property at $275,000, and every year you have reported a "loss" of $10,000, your taxable amount is reduced by $10,000 every year you owned the property. Assume you have been earning $100,000 annually from the property; the taxable income is pegged at $90,000. This example shows how depreciation is a real estate investor's hidden cash flow.

Equity Tax Benefits

The real estate market is associated with upward growth most of the time. Property tends to gain in value with only a few years when value and prices drop. On the time scale of 15-30 years, the value of the property you own is likely to go up. The loan portion of the property ownership structure also reduces thereby increasing the equity component.

It enhances the ratio between the property values of the loan. This means that you can refinance and pull equity from the property. The equity that you draw from the property is TAX-FREE. The idea is simple. The equity you pull is not income; it is a loan and therefore tax-free. Imagine of stocks. When you buy stocks, you have to sell the stocks and realize a profit or loss. You pay the tax on the profit you make.

This is considerably different in the case of real estate investment; you pull in equity in the form of a loan, and this is free of tax. In all this, you don't have to sell the property.

Tax Deductible Expenses

Real estate investment is a business just like any other. Unlike other forms of businesses, the expenses may not be direct. However, you have the opportunity to count them as expenses. When you get out looking for a property, all the costs you incur are tax deductible, including the vehicle expenses incurred. The same goes for expenditures related to repairs, painting, plumbing, security, property management among others.

All these costs are tax deductible from the rental income. All you need is to consult a qualified tax expert to determine what is tax deductible or not.

Tax Credit Benefits

There are several tax credits that you get by investing in properties and property related businesses. Take the following examples:

- 10% tax credit for the rehabilitation of any building that was placed in service on or before 1936

- 20% tax credit for rehabilitation of certified historic structures.

When renovating an office building, you enjoy a tax credit if you make the property wheelchair user accessible. For more details on benefits, see the IRS website. The incentives discussed so far are just general and may not be applicable in your particular circumstance.

Real Estate Investing Through REITs

There is another option through which you can get into the real estate market. This is very similar to the stock market. It involves buying the real estate investment trusts, just known as REITs. REITs, just like stocks, are purchased through brokerage accounts.

REITs are unique in very many ways. First, they operate under favorable tax structure. The tax structure in which REITs fall was created with the target being to encourage small investors that are unable to own properties to get into the real estate market.

In such arrangement, the REITs companies collect money from investors. The money is used to buy property (Income REITs or I-REITs) or develop properties (development or D-REITs). The properties into which the REITs can invest in include residential properties, shopping centers, hotels, industrial parks, go-downs, and any other commercial buildings and tracts of lands.

The corporates that go into REITs pay no Federal taxes as long as they abide by some requirements. They have to distribute at least 90% of their profits earned to the shareholders in the form of dividends. Unlike the companies, the real estate investment trust companies do not enjoy the same flexibility in determining their dividend payout policy.

However, REITs have their downside. They don't pay qualified dividends like stocks. In other words, once the investor is paid the dividend, the tax that applies is dependent on the investor's personal tax rate.

Investing in Real Estate through Home Ownership

Are you fed up with paying your landlord's mortgage, but are a little bit afraid of the commitment of buying your home? It's true; home ownership is a big responsibility. But it's also incredibly rewarding, and now is a good time to buy.

Long-term property ownership is pretty much the most guaranteed investment there is. With very few exceptions, real estate appreciates at a progressive rate. The market always has ups and downs, but the big picture it's that real estate always gains in value, so owners that sit on their investment for ten years or more are sure to earn equity that makes the endeavor worthwhile. Investing in real estate gives you long-term financial stability and independence.

Homeowners make the community. When people are financially invested in their community and have the long-term vision associated with real estate ownership, they are more committed to their community. When homeowners get involved in community events and neighborhood organizations, it builds the community and is rewarding for everyone involved.

Home ownership gives you creative control. You can decorate your surroundings however you want, and pets are always allowed--if you want them. If you are this type that loves to putter around the house and yard, you will love knowing that the work you do is increasing the value of your home and property and that you will be able to enjoy for as long as you want.

Another great reason to buy a home is that you can extend your mortgage to a long run and pay less per month, or speed up the process so that you pay more now, but are finished paying it back sooner. If you're a workaholic now but dream of an early retirement, this could be a great opportunity. Once your mortgage is paid off, that's it: the home is yours. You're just paying for insurance and utilities.

Even if you are a long away from paying off your mortgage, the average mortgage payment is far below what the same home or apartment would earn through rental income. Consider couples I know whose total monthly mortgage and insurance costs are at just around $700. The house they live in could rent for $1500 or more at their local rates. They're very glad they bought when they did.

So if you're sitting on the fence, considering buying, but a little wary of today's market, realize this: It's the right time to buy because the recent federal takeover of the two most important investment loan firms means low mortgage rates. Plus, with a market that's bottomed out, you know the only way home values are going to go at this point is up.

Risks of Real Estate Investing

A substantial percentage of returns from real estate are generated from leverage. In most cases, the investor acquires the property partly in equity and partly in debt. The percentage financed by equity is what the investor owns, and debt finances the rest.

As long as the returns are high enough, the investor can pay the amount due (part of principal and interest outstanding) and retain something for own use. However, if the market conditions are not right, and the returns are not being realized as expected, the investor can get into deeper problems than an investor who chooses to invest in a fully financed stock portfolio.

Conservatively, consider a debt-equity ratio of 50-50 when investing in real estate. There are extreme cases where investors opt for 100% equity. With a good selection of properties and assets included in the portfolio, the returns will be good even in a 100% equity structure arrangement.

Some Final Thoughts on Real Estate Investing

What you have learned so far are just the basics. There are several things you are going to learn as you start off. It is a journey that takes several years before you can be considered a professional.

If you are inexperienced, it is inadvisable to buy the property in your name. You are better off registering a limited liability company under which you can then purchase the property. This shields the investor from the personal liability should something go wrong.

As your portfolio grows to a significant value, you may consider setting up a real estate holding company. Also when buying property long-term consider events like death. In some countries inheritance tax is paid on your house when you die by whoever the house is passed to. In the UK for instance the surviving relatives pay 40% tax to the government. So consider this before you finance a house for 25 years or get into real estate. You must think of tax when you invest in real estate.

Significant returns can be achieved on real estate, but it should be remembered that house prices can fall as well as rise and that house letting can be a frustrating and expensive enterprise if the wrong tenants take up residence. Nevertheless, bricks and mortar are likely to continue to be popular for those who are interested in investing in the property market, particularly in the field of long-term investment.

Chapter 6: How to become a market wizard like Warren Buffet

Investing

Okay, let's be honest many of us will not become the next Warren buffet as it's simply not realistic. However, you can learn how many people make hundreds of thousands if not millions in the stock market. This chapter we will look at various ways you can leverage investments like the pro's do. As the financial markets can be risky for novices, I would highly advise you get professional advice and invest in training before going near the stock market.

Until the credit crunch in the late 1990's, followed swiftly by the recession, which affected most of the world's economies, investing cash in a bank to derive an income through interest was considered amongst the most efficient - and safest - ways of producing a return.

The collapse of many major banks exposed the myth that money invested in banks was always safe. The rapid reduction in interest rates in order to stabilize the world financial systems had an equally devastating effect on the notion that investing in a cash savings account produced a reliable source of income.

The rates of interest now offered by most savings institutions are so low that they are not keeping up with the rate of inflation. This means that, over time, your savings pot will become smaller and smaller, as interest does not keep up with the cost of living. Interest rates do not show any sign of increasing in the foreseeable future, so it appears that cash savings accounts are likely to remain a relatively poor means of investing our money.

The greatest advantage is that, compared to other vehicles, bank accounts are still considered to be the safest haven for our funds.

Stocks and Shares

Probably the investment model that causes the most trepidation to savers is the stock market. While it is undoubtedly the riskiest, carrying the possibility of the total loss of an investment, it usually provides the highest rewards.

As long as risk is spread evenly and stable, reliable advice is obtained, and an investor can ride out some short term losses, investment returns that beat the rate of inflation easily can provide a steady monthly or annual income.

With less hassle than investing in the property market, while carrying the potential for higher returns than cash savings, but with much more risk, investing in stocks and shares is not to be taken lightly and is most suitable for those who are willing to invest their money over the medium to long term.

Investing in Stocks for Beginners

Stocks are customarily referred to as the capital that is obtained by a company by selling shares. This form of investment is one that is accompanied by significant risks. But with this high-risk level comes the potential however to accumulate enormous wealth. Companies use stocks to raise cash. Stocks are simply ownership of part of a company. Compared to real estate the stock market is more complicated. In the stock market you can also buy leveraged positions (options, futures, CFDs etc.)

Create an objective

Initially, before exploring on the stock market, you will need to ensure that you have clearly defined your objectives or goals, whether mentally or written. This would include what you hope to achieve, whether it may be a long term or short term basis. Also, you would concisely show how much money and time you are willing to put into your investment. This consideration should not be taken lightly since you are now journeying into 'risky business.'

Getting down to Business

Defining your objectives might not pose much of a challenge. However, getting down to business and executing a plan will. It can be difficult studying the market, whether to ascertain when to buy stocks or when to sell them. Since the stock market consists of favorable (high) and unfavorable (low) periods, it can be difficult to decide what to do with your stock. It is ideal to purchase shares at the end of a decline and sell them after an increase in the market has stopped. This might seem simple, but many investors allow greed to prevail and so they make wrong choices such as buying when they should have been selling stocks. By studying the movements of stock prices on the stock chart, you will avoid becoming disappointed.

Continue Researching

The stock market is not constant. As such, things will always be changing. In this regard, it is vital that you continue to peruse the market. Ensure that you research a company thoroughly before endeavoring to invest in that company. Not only should you mull over the financial standing of the company, but you should also ponder over other non-financial details such as the company's image, their regularity and how well they operate.

Always ensure that you keep abreast of the market and remain on top of your game. Whether you decide to manage your money or employ someone, it's solely up to you.

There are some points that you must know about stock investing:

- It is not stock, but a company which you are buying.

- 100 percent of your assets should never be in stocks.

- The environment of the company influences the price of the stock.

- Your common sense and logic are as important as the advice of an investment expert in choosing the right stock.

- Use stop-loss orders, if you don't have any idea about the prospects of a company.

Here are some simple steps.

Step 1:

Get the big picture. To be successful in stock trading you will need to have a good understanding of macroeconomics. In other words, and understanding of the world economy and the local economy you are resident. You need to understand the difference sectors within that economy and how each sector is likely to react to economic factors. This is what investors call the big picture. If the interest rate is raised or lowered, what sectors are impacted the most? How is the dollar doing? Where will the dollar be in 6 months and how will it affect stocks? Understanding how the big picture works allows you to decide what sector of the economy you should buy stocks in. Once you have done this, you are ready for the next step.

Step 2:

Once you have picked a sector of the economy you think will do well (or even poorly) it's time to decide what stocks are the strongest candidates to pick within that sector. There are two types of analysis you can use to make an informed decision.

A: Technical Analysis

This is the mathematical analysis of price and volume data to determine if a stock is trending in price. In technical analysis the mathematical constructs used to determine if a stock should be purchased are called indicators or oscillators. There are many indicators you can research such as:

i)   Bollinger bands

ii)   Moving Averages
iii)   52-week high
iv)   52-week low
v)   MACD (moving average convergence)
vi)   Relative Strength indicator

These are but a few indicators that can be used for trend analysis. Some traders use technical analysis exclusively without studying the specific details of the company. Other traders use TA specifically to time their trades and have other methods of stock picking that determine what to buy and only use TA to determine when to buy. Technical trend data is normally presented as charts. If you are not familiar with TA, please read up more about it as it would take an entire book to go into the details.

B: Fundamental Analysis

This is when investors pick stocks based on company reports and financial data. The aim of FA is to access the company's health relative to its peers and determine if it is a strong candidate for future growth. Investors that use this tactic are called value investors. Here are a few terms that are commonly used in FA.

i)   Accounts Payable
ii)   Accounts Receivable
iii)   Acid Ratio
iv)   Amortization
v)   Assets - Current
vi)   Assets - Fixed
vii)   Book Value
viii)   Business Model
ix)   Business Plan
x)   Capital Expenses

xi)   Cash Flow

xii)   Cash on hand

xiii)   Current Ratio

xiv)   Customer Relationships

xv)   Days Payable

xvi)   Days Receivable

xvii)   Debt

xviii) Debt Structure

xix)   Debt: Equity Ratio

xx)   Depreciation

xxi)   Derivatives-Hedging

xxii)   Discounted Cash Flow

xxiii) Dividend

xxiv)   Dividend Cover

xxv)   Earnings

xxvi)   EBITDA

xxvii) Economic Growth

xxviii) Equity

xxix)   Equity Risk Premium

xxx)   Expenses Good Will

xxxi)   Gross Profit Margin

xxxii) Growth

xxxiii) Industry

xxxiv) Interest Cover

xxxv)   Investment

xxxvi) Liabilities - Current

xxxvii) Liabilities - Long-term

xxxviii)   Management

xxxix) Market Growth

xl)   Market Share

xli)   Net Profit Margin

xlii)   Page view Growth

xliii) Page views

xliv)   Patents
xlv)   Price/Book Value
xlvi)   Price/Earnings
xlvii)   PEG
xlviii) Price/Sales
xlix)   Product
l)   Product Placement
li)   Regulations
lii)   R & D
liii)   Revenues
liv)   Sector
lv)   Stock Options
lvi)   Strategy
lvii)   Subscriber Growth
lviii)   Subscribers
lix)   Supplier Relationships
lx)   Taxes
lxi)   Trademarks
lxii)   Weighted Average Cost of Capital

Once you are financially educated you may choose to use exclusively either Technical or Fundamental Analysis or maybe a hybrid of both. It will take practice and experience before you settle on a style that suits you. Contrary to what you might have read in other books the stock market is not as easy as you think and you need to first invest in your financial literacy before you invest a single dollar in the market.

Step 3:

 Investing is all about taking risk. To succeed you will need to learn how to manage risk, so you stay an active player in the game long enough to win. After stock picking portfolio management is arguably the most important skill you need. You need to manage both losses and wins. There is a huge psychological component to trading as in the heat of battle, traders can act very irrationally when there is money at stake.

Step 4:

Now you are ready to invest. So far, you have invested in your education and know all about economics and stocks. You are also a master of trade psychology and now how to manage yourself and your portfolio. Now you are finally ready to start small.

How to get started (putting it together)

The first thing that you should do is to determine the amount of money that you are willing to invest in the market. To be safe, you should invest small sums of money that you can afford to lose.

You should then ask your financial adviser to set up a brokerage account for you. The primary purpose of his counsel is to advise you on what you need to do. The adviser will also let you know about current market trends. If you don't want to make the trade decisions yourself then maybe you should look into mutual funds. Your adviser should be able to advise you on the various mutual funds available and can trade on your behalf if you prefer.

Decide on the stock to invest in

After setting up an account, you should take a decision on the stock to buy. When choosing the stock, you should think about the duration that you want to stay in the market. If you are planning on staying for a year or less, you should go for a stock that has the potential of growing quickly.

A great way of going about it is buying stocks from a company that is offering its initial public offering (IPO). To make money, you should get in right away and then sell the stocks a few days or months later when the price goes up.

Another great way of finding a stock that will rise in value quickly is to go for a company that is about to do a stock split. When stocks are divided, the value tends to rise fast; therefore, it's wise to buy the stocks before the split and then sell them when the price rises.

If you are planning on staying in the market for a long time, you should go for a company that has been in operation for a long time. The company should also have a good reputation of paying dividends. While it will take you more time to make money with this type of company, the stocks you buy are at less risk.

How to buy and sell stocks

You can buy and sell stocks using your broker, or you can do so on your own. If you don't have the skills on how to do it, it's wise to use your broker; however, if you have the skills you can go ahead and buy and sell the stocks on your own. These days most brokerage firms have apps you can download that allow you to manage your portfolio from the comfort of your phone.

Shares or stocks of a company always tend to go up and down, but over the long haul seem to do so much better than your average savings account. The main reason is that each stock within your investment portfolio has the potential to increase or grow in value. For example, if a company you have invested in is doing well, this also appreciates the value of its stocks or shares and therefore can be sold for more making you a profit.

On the other hand, those of us looking to create an additional stream of income can also turn towards stocks that pay out a dividend, which is monthly or annual payouts to shareholders.

Now the main allure of the stock market and investing has to be the chance of grabbing up the right stock, at the right time. Which can be done with proper research and of course dumb luck? Investing in the market today has to be one of the greatest ways to build wealth. From time to time any given company, which seems to be on the up and up, can suffer significantly from its industry or sector when demand brings to flounder.

Here is a scenario you often see in the market. Retail investors hear about new products or companies in the newspaper, on TV or the internet. And believing in the success of this product or company they begin to invest their money by buying stocks. The price rises and more and more retail investors pour in as this stock has become popular.

A few months later an unanticipated event happens and the stock drops steeply. This spooks the novice investor and they start to pile out of the stock, but can't find the liquidity to sell their stock so they lower their asking prices further fueling the drop in price. Then they repeat this same process over and over again until they have nothing left in their portfolio. Some may be lucky and hit a home run and become millionaires but eventually if they keep trading they will lose everything.

On the other hand, there are investors who are not looking to score home runs immediately. They analyze a stock and know that over the next 5, 10, 15 years the outlook for the company is good so they are disciplined and ignore the wild swings in market volatility, that happen from time to time. This is what value investors like Warren Buffet do, they read up everything they need to know about a company, they pick stocks and sit on them for sometimes decades before exiting with monstrous returns.

Investing in Bonds for Beginners

As you may know, bonds are typically considered to be one of the least risky investments available.

Bonds are loans that you give to a company (corporate), a city (municipal) or the U.S government (Treasury). These loans, for the most part, come with a guaranteed rate of interest, otherwise known as a coupon, along with a guaranteed date of return also known as the maturity date.

Now different types of bonds, like corporate bonds, are more lucrative than others. Due to a company's high risk of default, corporations tend to offer higher coupon rates on their bonds. This is extremely beneficial to you as the investor of course. Also, the length of the maturity date classifies what type of bond it is. For example, when you purchase a bond from the U.S government that takes less than a year to mature it would be known as a Treasury bill (or T-bill).

On the other hand, the bonds that are sold by corporations and mature less than a year are typically called commercial paper bonds. There are numerous types of bonds, notes, and bills that have to be taken into account.

The first step when you are thinking about investing in bonds is to decide where you want to invest and the strategy you want to use. There are a variety of different options to consider when you are investing in bonds, so there is a need to carry out thorough research and determine the best strategy that fits your goals.

Individual Bonds

Individual bonds are the basic types of bonds (the right types to get you started). Bonds sold in the over-the-counter (OTC) market are usually sold in specific denominations with $5,000 denomination being the most common. Bonds sold in the secondary market typically include a markup, which includes the dealers' profits and costs as well. If the bond isn't in the inventory, there could be additional costs because the dealer has to try and find these specific bonds.

Bond Funds

Bond funds are very similar to individual bonds, but your portfolio is professionally managed. The investor can then choose to diversify their bond investments and widen the variety. Bond funds don't typically have a maturity date because the investor is continually adding and eliminating bonds from their investment portfolio.

Bond Unit Investment Trusts

Bond unit investment trusts include a fixed portfolio of investments in municipal, mortgage-backed, government, and also corporate bonds that are professionally chosen and remain consistent throughout the life of the bond. The portfolio remains stable, which is a major advantage of a unit trust. This also allows you to know how much you can attain throughout the investment.

Money Market Funds

Money market funds are short-term pooled investments. They are highly liquid as well. The funds are made of the treasury bonds, the municipal bonds, the Treasury bills, the commercial papers and deposits with banks. The bonds are usually of the short-term nature, not exceeding two years in most cases. As a result of investors being able to withdraw their money at any time, this type of investment offers convenient liquidity.

The Approach

The strategic approach can be as simple as diversifying the bonds you purchase and then use those gains to reinvest and buy more bonds. Another option would be to purchase bonds that have a lengthy date of maturity because these types of bonds tend to yield higher returns from your initial principle. So remember that the variety of bonds available and their maturity dates are critical when it comes to mapping out your strategy to get rich from buying bonds. Also the amount of money you put into each bond plays a part in how soon you reach your financial goals.

Take into consideration that some companies only allow a minimum purchase amount. So in other words, to recap, your capitalization from bonds is determined from the sum of money that you're willing to lend and the period in for which you will invest it.

Some of you may say to yourself "I don't have enough principle to invest with." But, there are other ways for you to start building up your capital so that you can start taking progressive steps to riches.

In fact, there is an opportunity available to you that will allow you to earn money with very little risk! It's an investment vehicle that produces better returns than bonds.

The Investment Opportunities in Mutual Funds

What Are Mutual Funds?

Mutual funds are described as the professionally managed investment pools that bring together some securities, including stocks, treasury bonds, treasury bills, corporate bonds, commercial papers, fixed deposits, call deposits, and exchange traded funds, derivatives and real estate investment funds among other securities. A professional fund manager invests in one or more of these different security types to achieve the shareholders' specific investment goals.

Mutual funds allow investors to own shares in a pool of investments, thereby owning shares and bonds without incurring the risks associated with such shares directly.

The value of the assets in mutual funds is calculated at the end of every trading day to find the fund's net asset value. The mutual funds can be organized around specific securities.

The mutual funds bring together investors from far and wide, the small investors and the big investors. The investment manager takes charge of the investment decisions on a day to day basis, allowing the investors to concentrate on other things.

Most investors consider recent performance when choosing a mutual fund to invest their money. However, the investment/financial magazines, the fund rating agencies, investment T.V shows and other agencies also have a significant influence on investors when choosing a mutual fund.

The past performance of a mutual fund is a good indicator, but it is far from a guarantee. If you are looking for a long term investment, you will need to evaluate past performance. But lightening hardly strikes the same place twice. Consequently, you can get misled if you concentrate too much on history without considering other important factors. For example, during the tech boom of the 90's a mutual fund that was heavily weighted with tech stock probably did better than most. But during the crash all those gains were wiped away. Imagine if you invested in a mutual fund based on prior performance only for the mutual fund to tank a few months after. This is where you need to be sophisticated as an investor. Don't just pick a mutual fund because it has great recent history. Look into the mutual fund as far back as you can find data, investigate who the fund managers are. What other funds have they worked for and what was the performance?

Income Funds

Income funds attempt to balance higher returns against the high risks associated with the underlying assets. In most of these funds, the money is invested in a mix of assets. The funds may hold different proportions of equities and fixed income securities like bonds.

These funds have higher risks when compared to fixed income funds, but lower risks in comparison to pure equity funds. Each fund in this category has its goal. In some cases, the fund manager's approach may be more of equities and few bonds and vice versa. It is all about balancing the risk and the returns.

Bond Funds

These are funds that focus on long-term bonds for returns. In the recent past, bond funds have done very well, mainly due to the declining interest rates. However, this may not always be the case; bond funds are very volatile. Minor changes in the interest rates may have a significant impact on bond funds.

Balanced funds

Balanced funds put together a mixture of stocks and bonds in an equal or close to equal proportions. This is based on the evidence, and the widespread belief that the conditions that are favorable to the common stocks may not be favorable to bonds and the conditions that are favorable for bonds are equally unfavorable to the common stocks.

Money Market Funds

Money market securities target investors looking for short-term, but predictable income. They are also associated with low risks and low returns. It is a good fund to keep money and protect against inflation.

Treasury Bills

Treasury bills (T-bills) are highly liquid securities with very low bid/ask spreads. Securities are also exempted from the municipal and the state taxes. Treasury bills make a big portion of the asset composition of most money market funds. However, investors can also get into treasury bills directly by purchasing them directly from the government department.

Why Should You Consider Investing in Mutual Funds?

Mutual funds offer investors a way to park their investments or savings (the surplus money) in an investment scheme that meet their needs.

If you have time, resources and skills required in the field of investment, try your luck in the stock market, bond market or other high-risk investment opportunities.

However, not all of us have all that time to dedicate resources researching and observing how the companies perform, the performance of industries and the economy so as to determine which particular stocks have good prospects.

It is precisely for this reason that many people find it profitable to hand over their savings to a well-established and experienced professional to take charge and manage the investment process. The investment managers pool together resources from many investors/savers and invest the funds in a pool. How exactly do you benefit from mutual funds?

Grow your golden eggs through a systematic process: Systematic investment process is where an investor saves/invests a particular amount periodically. It is the most preferred method when saving for a retirement plan. In this way, the investor consistently tops up his/her savings. As time goes, the investor enjoys the benefits of the bullish and the bearish markets as well.

Focuses on the long-term financial goals: In the mutual funds, there is always a scheme for all clients. These include equity funds, fixed income/bond funds, money market funds, balanced funds among others. Depending on your risk versus return appetite, you can find a fund to put your investment. The investors interested in short-term schemes are better off with the money markets. Either way, your financial advisor and the fund manager will advise you to invest in the appropriate fund subject to your needs.

How much should you invest?

Identify your cash inflows and outflows: when trying to figure out how much to put in the mutual funds, you need to know how much surplus you have. It is the surplus that you can afford to invest. To calculate your surplus, subtract the outflows from the inflows. A positive balance is the amount of money you can invest.

A negative balance on the other hands means that you need to borrow to finance the extra expenses. However, a negative balance could also be an indicator that you need to adjust your expenses so that you live within your means.

That is a personal finance lesson for another day. All the same, you have to manage your income and expenditure so that you have something to save in the mutual funds after catering for your primary/basic needs as well as the non-basic needs.

Managing a mutual fund investment

You have to monitor the existing investments closely: It is often said that the mutual funds provide returns in the long run. This might be true, but it does not give an investor a reason to invest and forget everything.

If you want to maintain a balanced return, it is important that you review your investments and adjust the investment plan should there be a need. Fund managers will do their best to balance the securities so as to maximize the returns to the investor.

However, the investor has the duty to carefully monitor and compare the actual returns against the promised returns and make the adjustments thereafter. You may want to compare your mutual fund against the mutual funds in the industry.

If you have a portfolio, this is the best way to remove the underperforming mutual funds in your portfolio. You don't have to keep the mutual funds if you are not getting any value from it. Comparing performance is not that difficult. It's all about comparing the mutual fund returns in percentages.

What Mistakes to Avoid when Investing in Mutual Funds

To get to your investment destination and meet your investment objectives, you need a less volatile investment journey. Having 100% gains one year followed by a 95% loss the next is not the performance you need. Yes, you may be lucky to get two or even three consecutive years of high returns but if performance is volatile it only takes one year of bad performance to wipe out all your profits. So rather than looking for extremely high returns, look for returns with a proven track record of consistency over time.

This is only possible if you avoid the mistakes most people make when investing in mutual funds.

Investing without an investment goal and a financial plan in place

If you are going to invest in a mutual fund, you need a plan. This is so basic, but your investment is likely to fail if you don't have a plan. There are many goals that could influence your investment plan, these could be the goal of buying a car, a house, wedding costs, tuition, saving for your children, the list is endless. Your goals will determine if you should invest in short or long-term timeframes and what acceptable risk should be.

Investing without a budget

Investing without a plan and a budget is like trying to fly a plane without enough fuel. The key to succeeding in investment is that you supercharge the power of compounding, by periodically adding more money to your investments.

Without a clear plan you will find this difficult to achieve as you must have clear and concise control of incoming and outgoing cashflow before you can determine what the surplus disposable income is.

Not having a plan may lead to you being short of cash and having to liquidate positions prematurely which will hurt you in the long run.

You want to continue investing every month without running out of cash and getting tempted to withdraw part of what you have invested so far. This is like crash landing when you run out of fuel. To avoid impulse buying and the emotional spending, you need to explicitly enumerate the areas which you expect to spend on, categorize them into essential and non-essential and consider what can be avoided.

This is simply a cash flow plan; it captures the areas of cash inflows and outflows. When dealing with projections, it is called a budget. It is best done in excel on your P.C. It guides your spending. With the required disciple and conservative approach to spending, you should be able to save as much as 20% of your income. The other possible sources of income include gifts, bonus, lottery wins and inheritance among others.

The more savings you make now, the better your future. Investing is a way of compounding your earnings while growing the value of your assets in the future.

Investing with no clear understanding of the risk-return

I was watching a show the other day on TV. The show was about people who bid blindly on storage units that had been repossessed due to non-payment. The highlight of the show was when someone bid maybe $100 for a lot and after paying discovered there was a rare collector's item worth $10,000 - $50,000, but the reality is for every one of these great buys televised there are another 99 that these punters lose money (just like the stock market).

In the case of this TV shows the buyers accepted the risk of not knowing what they were getting, for the chance of winning big. In mutual funds and trading in general not knowing the risk can lead to bankruptcy.

So you must understand the risk, but also understand the expected timeframes for returns. For instance, will you need the money back in 6 months, 5 years or 10 years?

Here is a simple rule of thumb, if you do not need the money in the next five years; you can consider investing it in equity mutual funds. If the money is needed within the next five years, it would be better to invest in the bond and fixed income funds. If the money will be needed within the next six months or year, investing in the money market is the best option.

Consider taking a profiling test. Most financial planners will give you the risk profiling test. It does not last more than 20 minutes.

You get to know your risk profile through such tests. The risk profiles are categorized into cautious, conservatives, moderate and aggressive risk takers. The user profile determines the percentage of your assets that should go to equity, bonds/debt instruments, or the liquid funds like the money market.

Investing without adequate research

A person who proceeds to invest without the basic research is like the individual who starts a car and drives without knowing where he is going. The generally accepted philosophy holds that you should never buy an item without doing research and compare it with similar items regarding quality, prices, and its necessity. This rule also applies to mutual funds. The requirements vary, though.

It is advisable to spread your investment/savings in not more than 3 or 4 well-performing mutual funds. Too many mutual funds increase paperwork, and no one wants to waste too much time comparing funds and dealing with different fund managers.

Comparing Real Estate, Stock, and Gold: The Ideal investment portfolio for you

Should I choose Real estate or the Stock market?

There is no simple answer to this, so let's have a closer look at both. Your investment profile will be determined by your knowledge and experience and how much disposable income you have.

Stock Markets

They are very volatile, but a decent way of building wealth. In the stock market you can see investments jump 10 fold in one month. But the reverse is also true, you can invest in stocks and lose everything in hours. The stock market is risky for all those who are hasty and inexperienced.

The key to making money in the stock markets is controlling risk and having discipline. The problem with the stock market is that many people get lucky and see their $10,000 turn to a million overnight and many investors pile in looking for fool's gold.

But where there is risk there is also reward. If you invest in financial education and you are willing to take your time and start small until you master the craft of stock investing, you can do really well for yourself. The problem is we all want to be the next Warren Buffet overnight. If you set realistic goals and acquire the requisite experience and skill, there is no reason you can't make it with stocks.

Pros

High Returns – as stated above you can really make killer returns in the stock market. Should you learn how to use leveraged instruments like options and futures you can get returns of 1000% + within a single year (but you can also lose more than you invested). Stock trading has to be one of the most lucrative investment vehicles there is.

Cons

High Volatility – If high returns represent all that is great about the stock market, volatility must be the evil twin most people don't know about. Volatility is not inherently good or bad as it's only an indicator of how likely the price of an asset will change in time. But uncontrolled risk mixed with volatility is what cripples stock traders. You cannot afford to take your eye off the ball. Many people have lost their entire life savings in the stock market, sometimes in as little time as a single year. Leveraged instruments (naked options, futures, etc.) are also very dangerous as brokerages allow you to borrow money / stock to buy a bigger position than you can afford (this is called margin). If the position goes against you, then you will not lose just your capital but also the money you borrowed to buy the stock.

You should avoid leveraged positions for several years, until you have built up the skill, discipline and experience to handle leverage and volatility.

Real Estate Markets

The great thing about Real estate is that it is sure to produce returns on your investment. It is notoriously tough for first-time investors (who often don't have sufficient lines of credit and experience). However, do not let it prevent you from investing in real estate if you are only just starting out.

Investing in real estate assures you of stable and profitable returns over the years. The returns may not be as high as compared to stock markets but you can still make fairly decent returns and income. Unlike stocks you will never end up losing the entire value you invest as quickly as you can with stocks.

Pros

With real estate investment, you should be able to make your properties earn money beyond their overall value, assuming that you have people living in the property and paying rent. This means that your investment actively makes money at all times. Furthermore, there will always be a need for properties, so as long as you invest money wisely and know which areas are creating the highest levels of demand, you should be reasonably safe even if the market gets a little bit tumultuous.

Cons

While your property will make extra money for you if you have people renting them, the opposite is true as well. Property investments require maintenance. This means that you have to spend a little to make sure it is in good shape before the property goes to the market.

Furthermore, your cash will be tied into a property, so it is not instantly accessible. To get to it, you will often have to wait weeks, or even months, for sales to be completed and all of the paperwork to be filled out. So think about liquidity before plunging into real estate.

Investing in Gold

Gold has been the traditional store of wealth for centuries. Paper currencies were only invented as a way to make gold transactions easier. The promissory note (currency) was called a legal tender, which meant you were able to walk up to a bank and demand gold in exchange for your promissory note (that you 'tendered').

In the current world economy, the dollar has now become the accepted global currency. But it's worth noting that the United States of America may lose this position as bearer and printer of the world's number one currency. Investors often suffer from experience bias i.e. because house prices have always gone up, they believe that houses will rise indefinitely without correction (because they have not experienced anything else). Many also believe the dollar will always be the world currency. All I will say on this is research what happened to the Great British Pound as the world number one currency after war and debt crippled the UK's economy several decades ago. Could history repeat itself?

Pros

Gold is a tangible asset and, in the current economy; it is only going to continue to increase in value. As long as the government (USA) is printing more money, your gold should become a more and more profitable investment.

Furthermore, once you have purchased your gold, you don't need to do anything beyond waiting for the most opportune time to sell it. It requires no maintenance or additional investment, meaning you can often make a tidy profit quite quickly, assuming you play the market right.

Cons

There is no real way to make some additional money from your gold, so it is literally dead weight until such a time as it is advantageous to sell. While this is not a problem from a safety perspective, it means you aren't making as much money as you might otherwise make (lazy money).

You'll also find it is much harder to negotiate the price of gold downwards, as the market tends to be pretty set when you come to buy. Couple that with the fact that you will often need to pay an additional percentage of the purchase to a dealer on top and you may find your gold costs more as an initial investment than you are comfortable with.

Over the past 15 years many have accurately depicted and analyzed the fall of the dollar. The economic data suggests that the dollar will soon lose its place but it's difficult to make this play, as no one can predict with accuracy exactly when this will happen.

The dollar might collapse this year or it might still hold on for another twenty years. Nobody really knows, but if you follow respected gold enthusiasts like Jim Rogers and Peter Schiff, you get a feeling that it is imminent.

Conclusion – What should you invest in?

Nobody can tell you what the right investment for you should be. Even a dead clock is right twice a day, so pay no attention to market predictions. The truth is nobody can predict the markets with any degree of replicable certainty. Investing is not about predicting.

It's about probability and risk. Investing is about trying to ascertain trends. Trends are more predictable over longer periods than shorter timeframes (this is why Warren Buffet is successful). For instance, Warren can't predict what the price of Coca-Cola stock will be next year but he knows that based on historical data that Coca-Cola will most likely double or triple or quadruple in ten years.

This is how smart investors tame the market. Looking at the market through the lenses of history will reduce the noise. Too many investors rush into investing based on temporal noise that is sometimes merely government (global) or market manipulation.

Whatever you choose in the end do me one favor, do your homework thoroughly and don't rush things. Remember how hard you worked for your money and work just as hard to keep it ☺

Chapter 7: How to make money while you sleep.
The power of Passive Income

In the last chapter we looked at some of the traditional wealth creation vehicles like real estate, stocks and even gold. But there are other ways to make money in this digital age that you may not be aware of. In this chapter we will look at some practical low-cost ways you can start a side business that can earn you enough income to quit your current job. Like with everything else in this book please read up more and invest in your education. So let's look at some ideas.

Passive Income - Affiliate Marketing

Affiliate marketing is a form of marketing technique in which the affiliate marketer takes the place of a promoter. In this way, the affiliate marketer/promoter helps the sellers and the manufacturers to connect and reach the end consumers. This is an easy online income generating activity in which you can opt to take an active role or choose to take a passive role. By all definitions, an affiliate marketer is not the producer, creator or origin of the products he/she is promoting. In the whole arrangement, the affiliate marketer earns a commission from each sale made through his link. It is a 3-way relationship between the manufacturer/originator, the affiliate marketer, and the end consumers.

Cutting through the crap and rubbish

As a frequent internet user, you will get unsolicited emails very often. Some of the emails will be asking you to join an affiliate network community. The catch is that you have to pay an upfront payment. Should this be the case, you have to be very careful. They could be a scam or legit, but how do you tell the scams?

The only real way to know if it is a scam or a legit email is to visit the Better Business Bureau (BBB). This provides all the information that you need about the company. The other alternative is to visit affiliate marketing forums and discussions from where you can get free testimonies and advice. News spread very fast, especially on the social media platforms.

The other common trend is where a marketer tries to sell you a product with catchy titles, but nothing substantial that can help you succeed in affiliate marketing.

It is easy to learn all you want to know about affiliate marketing from the top ranking websites, blogs, and good quality EBooks. Usually, it costs you nothing to become an affiliate. All you need is to sign up with one of the affiliate marketing programs.

However, you will have to spend a little in web hosting. This could cost from $70 to $100 every year. There are some other expenses most of which are optional. For instance, you may want a unique website or blog logo, or you may hire a blog writer, or even promote your site with advertising, all these are discretionary expenses.

How Many Types of Affiliate Marketing Exists?

The most interesting part of affiliate marketing programs is that there are more ways to earn income than most people imagine. The following are just a few examples:

Unattached Affiliate Marketing

The unattached affiliate marketing requires the least effort and very little work. The affiliate marketer does not need to setup an affiliate marketing blog like in the case of Amazon Affiliate Programs. It is as simple as the pay-per-click (PPC) where the entire affiliate marketer needs to do is to show the affiliate ads on a site. The affiliate marketer gets a commission from the traffic the Ad generates.

The Related Affiliate Marketing

This marketing requires some effort. The affiliate marketer needs to get involved by creating an affiliate marketing blog, a website or both. The marketer shows the affiliate links on his blogs and website. Web users click the ads/links, and this is how the marketer makes income.

Involved Affiliate Marketing

In this marketing technique, the affiliate marketer may have to try the product or service after which he/she writes a review on the product. In this case, the affiliate marketer earns a reputation by consistently writing excellent articles, comprehensive and honest reviews of the goods and services.

Affiliate Marketing Models

In addition to the three types of affiliate marketing, you also need to understand the different affiliate programs from which you can make money.

Pay per Click (PPC) Model: This is a very traditional model for affiliate marketing particularly for small websites. It is also the easiest method to earn money in online marketing. The affiliate marketer has to place a link to the product or service of the merchant on his/her website. The affiliate earns a commission every time a client visits the merchant's website through the link. The commission is based on the number of visitors, the commission paid is not great, and the affiliate only gets to earn a significant amount if massive traffic can be generated.

Pay per Sale Model: This is the most used model. In this case, the advertisers pay a commission every time they sell a product through the link created by the affiliate. The ad link is set up on the affiliate website if the website user clicks on the ad and goes ahead to buy the product/service, the affiliate earns a commission.

Pay per Performance (PPP): This is also very popular and is the highest paying model. In this model, the merchant pays the affiliate a commission if the affiliate's referrals translate into action. The actions could vary; the visitor referred through the link could buy a product or become a lead. The affiliate may earn anywhere from 15% to 20% of the total sales made.

Pay per Lead: This is a model that is commonly adopted by the insurance companies and related finance companies. The affiliate's role is to refer visitors to the merchant website and make sure that they fill out a form or provide some sought of personal information. The affiliate acts as the lead in this case.

Affiliate Marketing Categorization

Other than the main two types of classifications (related and unrelated), affiliate marketing programs are also categorized into the single tier, two tier, and the multi-tier. The single-tier program is where the affiliate gets paid for the direct sales or traffic into the merchant web page and nothing more. The two tier affiliate, allows the affiliate to earn from direct referrals as well as the indirect referrals; referrals made by the ones he recruited. The multi-tier program allows the affiliate to earn from a vast network.

Putting the Cogs and Wheels Together

With this introduction, you now have an idea of what affiliate marketing really is, the input required from you and the common pitfalls. Is this enough for someone who wants to start his journey into financial freedom?

Affiliate marketing is just like any other business opportunity and needs to be approached as such. It requires an elaborate plan that takes you from one day to the next, month to month and years to come.

With this reality in mind, it only makes sense to discuss the strategy you may need for you to become an affiliate marketer. The plan may include setting up a specialized blog if you decide to become an expert in niche of the product you are promoting. Let's look at some of the main considerations for your plan if you choose to explore affiliate marketing.

The Steps in Becoming an Affiliate Marketer

Decide on Niche Topic: It is important to take a decision on a specific topic that you want to discuss on your website. If you are going to write reviews on products or services, then the reviews should be for the products that you are really passionate about. This is a sure way to write better and honest reviews. It could be about fashion, toys, child bicycles, vehicles or hair products. These are just a few examples. Trust me; affiliate programs have huge product inventories, and you have to pick a few to market through your blogs or website.

Website and Webhosting: With the niche topic in place, you need to create a website and find a reliable web hosting service provider. Today, you can design your own website using WordPress, Web.com, eHost, and Blogger (among others). These online tools come with "click and drag" features through which you can design a website in a matter of minutes. However, you can also hire a reliable designer to complete the web design.

SEO: Learn the basics of SEO and how to use it to market your website and blog posts. SEO means search engine optimization. This is an important tool that you need to understand and take advantage of, if you want to make money as an affiliate marketer or online in general for that matter. It is a marketing strategy through which specific keywords are used to rank your website ahead of others so that users find your site first. It is a sure way of getting maximum traffic. More visitors translate to more sales and more money.

Social media in marketing: Social media marketing (SMM) is part of the SEO campaign. Your success online requires that you get involved in social media marketing. Most online users are part of the social media community. The platforms like Twitter, Facebook, Instagram, YouTube, Twitter, LinkedIn, Pinterest, Tumblr, Vine, Meetup, Ask.fm, Flickr, and VK among others can be of great help when marketing your blogs.

Paid Advertising: You need to learn about paid advertising, and decide if paid advertising should be part of your advertising campaign or not. With paid ads, you will be able to target the right people and the people in need of the specific products that you are promoting. This increases the chance of your visitors buying the products through the affiliate links.

You need content for your website: If you plan to get into an affiliate marketing blog, you must critically think of the blog posts you are going to include in your websites. The articles have to be very impressive to attract an audience. With boring articles, you will not get repeat readers. In fact, if you are going to write boring articles, forget about affiliate marketing via blogging. Does the article you write impress you? If yes, go ahead and post it, if no, reconsider everything. Please as explained previously you don't need to write a blog. Blogging is simply a way to get repeat organic website traffic you can sell to, over and over again.

If you don't like writing, you can simply just advertise the affiliate product on your site, but remember that users will need to have a reason for coming to your site in the first place. If you can generate traffic to your site by other means, please do so. Also consider outsourcing the content generation for your blog to freelance writers. A huge number of blogs are actually written by ghostwriters.

With good content, you will get more readers translating to high traffic. This will boost your earning capacity.

So, how do you earn from affiliate marketing?

Usually, a seller or a manufacturer (product owner) signs a partnership with an affiliate program/network. As an affiliate marketer, you will sign up with the affiliate network. You get to earn a commission on the products sold through your links.

This means that the affiliate has to embed/display the affiliate link on his blogs or web pages as a way to promote the products. It is this link that will guide the visitors to your blog, to the seller's page from where they can make the purchase.

The commission you earn from each sale is not very big. It can range from 1% to 10%. It is rare to get a commission above 10%. Consequently, you are only going to earn good money if you generate huge traffic to your blog or website, and you have a high sales conversion rate.

With informative reviews and articles, your readers are more likely to click on the links and make purchases.

Let's say that you earn a commission of $10 from every sale. This is not sufficient to convince you to become an affiliate writer. However, if you manage to get 20,000 visitors in your blogs in 30 days, and 10% of them purchase the goods, it comes down to 2,000 sales. With the commission of $10 per sale, you earn as much as $20,000 per month.

How much can you earn?

Well, there is no limit, that's the honest answer. There is no limit to how much you can earn. The earnings through affiliate marketing is limitless. Well, there are numerous examples of websites that have made as much as $50,000 per month within two years of operation. In your case, you can comfortably run 3 to 4 sites for affiliate marketing.

The answer as to how much you can make is a matter of your imagination. It is more to do with how much you are willing to put in, how hard you are willing to work and how much you want to earn.

I am very confident that you are ready to get started having read this topic. All you need is to create your websites and start posting excellent blog posts. After that, you will soon be talking about financial freedom with no life worries, if you can put in the work and further research required. Affiliate marketing like all other passive income requires work in the beginning to get things moving, but after a few months you will only need a few hrs. a week to maintain and manage your income.

Passive Income – E-Books

Before understanding the way in which an e-book writer creates content, you need to know what an EBook is and why it is so popular nowadays. E-book (electronic book) is the future of the publishing industry, and the internet has made it easy for anyone to publish an e-book and make money.

In comparison with paper books in the case of storage space, e-books require lesser physical space. E-book readers (Kindle, mobile phone, and tablet devices etc.) help you to read and carry many e-books. The number of e-books you can carry is dependent on the capacity of the device. The main case for e-books is the convenience it presents to book lovers. Here are a few of the other benefits

1. Easy storage and retrieval of books (on demand)
2. Faster delivery of books after purchase
3. Interactive content (allows hyperlinks)
4. Books can be borrowed digitally
5. Easier to publish for authors

In 2011 it was reported that sales of e-books had surpassed printed versions for the first time. These days you don't even need to buy a kindle device to read e-books as there are Apps on phones, tablets and even pc's that will allow you to purchase and read e-books very easily.

E-books can be written on any topic just like paper books. E-books can also be developed in fictional, non-fictional, biographical and referential subjects. So, how can I make money from this you ask? The two main ways to make money in this digital age is with independent publishing (Indy) and ghost writing. So you will either put a digital book together and sell it, or get paid to write books as a ghostwriter. It's worth noting that you don't need to be a writer to get into Indy publishing as many people who can't write themselves get ghostwriters to produce manuscripts.

Independent publishing

Starting as a freelance e-book writer can be a good choice for a lot of writers. In addition to generating revenue through e-book writing, it helps establish you as an authority in your chosen field of expertise. As an e-book writer, you must thoroughly understand your target audience and also the theme you have chosen so that clarity in expressing the topic can be achieved.

If you don't have an idea about, which theme to write about, conducting an internet search or asking people's views, can help you. Pick a subject, on which you can express your ideas clearly and precisely. You can begin with short stories or short articles before venturing into writing an e-book.

#1: Determine the Size of Your Market

It is important that you identify some market variables before you publish your eBook online, except you are writing for fun and pleasure and not to make money with eBooks. I know that there is nothing wrong being a writer who wants his voice to be heard by a target audience and not to make money online. But for selling authors, I know you want to make money writing eBooks. This is where determining the size of your market becomes vital.

You can use niche market forums, keyword research tools, and surveys, to find out what people want to read about and if it's within your area of expertise.

Get to know your potential buyers, the market demand and if they will be willing and able to buy your eBook.

#2: Learn How to Optimize Your Website

There is always cutthroat competition in every niche market; you venture into online now. There are no more obscure and profitable niches that have not been discovered anymore. So, for you to be ahead of the competition, you have to optimize your website (or publishing platforms i.e. amazon or iTunes listings) for target keywords related to your eBook idea. On-page SEO (search engine optimization) is crucial to your eBook marketing success because you will want free targeted traffic from the search engines (Amazon and Google).

#3: Be Ready to Market your eBook

From experience and observations, you will notice that successful eBook authors are aggressive marketers. It is common to recruit the affiliate marketers or enter into a joint venture partnership as long as it helps increase the sales. A lot of e-authors now turn to social media to reach as many potential buyers and clients as well. If you are lukewarm in your eBook marketing drive, there is little you can do to improve your eBook sales volume and ultimately make profits.

#4: Set the Right Price for Your eBook

You should set a competitive price for your electronic book that your target market can afford. This means you have to conduct market price research to know the average price that other authors are charging their customers. The only exception is when you are a well-known authority in your niche market, or you are convinced that you are bringing unique knowledge to the table.

#5: Write Attention-Grabbing Titles

To a large extent, the compelling and attention-grabbing title can go a long way to selling your eBook, and you can use it for branding purposes. An excellent eBook title will give you the clicks and opportunity to present your sales copy to your potential buyers.

You have two primary options to choose from when researching your electronic book title to use. The first choice is to select a keyword rich title and the second is to choose a benefit-rich title.

#6: Demonstrate Your Expertise

There are many ways to demonstrate and express your expertise in your niche subject before you publish your eBook online. Write an eBook and start distributing it for free. You can even use it to build an email list of subscribers before finally launching your product.

Another method of building your expertise and visibility is to write SEO articles and distribute through relevant internet media such as article directories, blogs, social media, and so on. You can also grant interviews to bloggers, experts, and webmasters in your niche market.

#7: **Write an Effective Sales Copy**

In your eBook marketing campaigns, there is no face-to-face selling. And because you are going to be directing potential buyers to your sales copy, it is important you take the time and extra care to craft something that will appeal to their emotions. You want them to see and appreciate the benefits of downloading your eBook more than the money they will pay for it.

You should read lots of good sales copies in your niche market and make notes of hot buttons in all these materials. You can now take notes on these top 7 ideas before you publish your eBook online.

How do you make money writing eBooks?

Most prolific writers will give you several reasons behind their eBook writing prowess. With eBooks, the writer does not have to worry about paper pages; the books are easy to format, and the ease of publishing them leaves the writers with more time to research and write more books.

But if you want to make a lot of money as an eBook writer then you need to be able to write fast. The faster you can produce an eBook the quicker you can start selling it, and you can go about selling it for years as long as the content is up to date. Even fiction books can get outdated sometimes.

So you need to create eBooks fast if you want to earn your living this way.

The first thing you have to do with any eBook is research your subject. Even fiction books sometimes need a bit of research to make sure they are factually correct.

Research can be done quickly on the internet. These days most libraries now have their reference books online too. Just make sure that you don't get distracted by websites that look attractive but have no relevance to your research. Stay focused. Set aside an amount of time for research and that way, you'll be less distracted by 'pretty' things you find on the internet because your time will be limited.

Next, you need to outline your eBook thoroughly so that you know exactly what information you're going to be including and in what order. Then it's time to start writing. If you've researched enough and outlined correctly, the actual writing should be easy and fast to do since you will have enough notes and outlines for referencing. You also have all the information still fresh in your mind.

Next, you need to make money from your eBook.

EBooks are written for different reasons. The most obvious reason is to sell it and make money. While writing is an excellent way to make money writing eBooks, there are other ways too.

PLR eBooks

If you do not want to write or outsource your books to ghostwriters, you can consider PLR.

PLR stands for Private Label Rights. This means the that book you are selling, has copyrights that is within the public domain.

This simply means that the book was written a number of years ago can be sold by anyone. The majority of PLR content available comes from books that were written several years ago and after the author died the rights to the book passed into the public domain.

So there are several classic books you can sell as the rights are PLR.

When someone releases a PLR eBook, it becomes theirs to do with as they please. The original content should not be altered or changed (infringement) but you can add additional content like diagrams, annotations, extra info about original author etc. The aim with PLR publishing is to take a classic and try to spice it up a little by adding some sort of value without infringing on the original content.

Many eBook writers sell only a certain amount of each PLR eBook so as not to flood the market with similar products.

Some eBook writers package their eBooks with promotional articles and a sales page to attract more buyers. The only problem with PLR eBooks is that if you're selling a limited number of each one, your income is finite, but you can charge a higher price per copy.

Promotional eBooks

Writing small promotional eBooks to be used as a giveaway when selling products is a common trend. Some of the eBooks are used as promotional materials for bigger eBooks, services or products. This is simply a viral marketing strategy. Everyone loves freebies. Consequently, the free eBook is likely to get downloaded thousands of times and then used in thousands of websites. The technique is excellent for promotion.

Promotional eBooks are also an excellent way to market not just your eBooks, but your websites too, and get you known as a leader in your niche. Promotion eBooks are like a Trojan horse for future upsells and marketing. In other words, we create free content and try and sell the buyers products later on.

Resale rights

This is similar to PLR except that your eBook cannot be changed in any way. Those who buy your eBook with resale rights, get the right to sell it themselves. Selling an eBook this way means you need to place strict terms for re-selling such as not undercutting you on price and not changing the eBook in any way. Selling an eBook with resale rights, unlike PLR, means you can go about selling it for years. This method is typically used to sell rights to your books in a foreign language. If you have a book and its doing well in English why not try publishing in French or at least sell the rights to a French publisher.

Make money with ghostwriting

If you find that you love writing eBooks and are good at it, you could hire yourself out as an eBook ghost writer. Writing eBooks this way means that you'll never get recognition for your work, but you will be paid for everything you write. It's not unusual for eBook ghost writers to charge several thousand dollars to write an eBook. Some authors have earned as much as $1,600 for writing a 10-page eBook.

Get Affiliates

You can use affiliates to help drive sales of your eBooks. Paying affiliates 50% commission or more is the norm. Try to get a super affiliate to sell your eBook and generate hundreds or even thousands of sales; it's wise to increase their commission to motivate them to sell even more eBooks for you. This method cannot be done with platforms like Amazon or Google books, but you should be able to achieve this using affiliate networking platforms like ClickBank.

Writing and Formatting EBooks

Ideally, 99% of your time ought to be spent on writing and advertising/marketing your eBook. Technically, an eBook is an electronic book, but you have to choose the right format. 99% of all eBooks are read and downloaded on Apple's iOS devices (iPhone, iPad and iPod Noble Nook, Amazon's Kindle and Barnes.

Converting your eBook in formats adapted by these eBook readers gives it better prospects for sales.

Formats for eBooks and eBook Software

Once you have your content created, there are many ways to publish the final product. The publishing industry has been turned upside down with the evolution of digital editions, eBooks, the rapid technology changes, and so much more. Now, instead of cracking open that new binding and having the faint new book smell, you have a clickable file that enables readers to access your content instantly. Now the daunting task of trying to decipher between different self-publishing eBook formats such as

HTML5, AZM, ePUB, and MOBI and which works best for your needs comes in.

ePUB- is one of the most popular formats out in the digital publishing world. It is an open standard format adopted by Barnes, Noble, and Apple. A list of other eBook reader makers such as Sony also supports EPub. First developed by the International Digital Publishing Forum, this format fits multiple devices except for Kindle. If you want a simple, non-media rich text format, then this format may be a simple self-service eBook publishing solution for you.

.mobi - is exclusively made by Amazon for Kindle, meaning that no other device can open this format. This is a great format if you are specifically and solely targeting the Kindle market, but does not allow for maximum reach like some of the others. Not to be confused with AZM, another eBook format which is a compressed version of .mobi exclusively made for Kindle. This format is viewable on more devices through an Amazon Kindle app.

HTML5- is the ultimate, all-inclusive eBook format. Because it's not designed for a particular e-reader, but rather any web browser on smartphones and tablets, it allows for universal visibility on all digital platforms. Not only is this format universal, but it allows for maximum reach as well as the interactive benefits of video and audio.

Utilizing eBook software will convert your eBook content into a digital interactive flipbook will enable you to create an HTML5 format as well as a flash based format for optimal computer viewing and have the best all-inclusive method of self-publishing your eBook.

You can then sell your content on your site without having to pay specific platforms a fee every time you sell your content. When using eBook software to convert your content, you should ensure that you have a high resolution, media rich, and stunning page flipping publication that is instantly clickable and viewable on all digital platforms.

PDF was originally designed for print. You can't really enjoy a vivid display of PDF content on digital devices. But PDF is a useful format if you're sending some data to an Android or iOS device. Kindle supports the PDF format.

What Kind of Book Makes the Best EBook?

All kinds of books can be converted to eBooks. The earlier notion that only books with text and some inline images are ideally suited for an eBook, no more hold true now. You can convert illustrated cookbooks, children's books, cookbooks and travel books to eBooks but it is a meticulous process.

However, a professional eBook conversion company can handle that easily. EBooks have a "killer feature" of increasing font size. It's a major factor to consider if you want your eBook to be a good sales product. Your book can instantly become a large type book. ePub supports animations, audio, videos and many more other enhancements too.

Why Outsource?

You can always save yourself from unnecessary hard work and expenses. Creating an eBook can be as easy as it can be if you outsource. Look for an eBook conversion company that offers the best value for your money. Some eBook conversion services translate Word document to EPub format at an inexpensive price. These services are affiliated with Amazon and Apple as well. Other than creating your eBook (formatting and conversion), they also submit it to these bookstores for a small fee.

There is easy DIY software to make your own eBooks. If you want to sell on Amazon's Kindle store, you'll find a handy guide for converting your Word file through the site's Kindle Direct Publishing (KDP) feature. It's free to create an account and use the service.

They often say not to judge a book by its cover, but in the eBook world aesthetics are really important. So take care of how the book looks and how well it was put together as readers are allowed to read the first 10% for free on many platforms before making a final buying decision.

EBook Covers: How to go about it?

Let's start with why an eBook cover is critical to get readers to purchase your great eBook:

How many times do you find yourself judging an eBook by its cover? If you are like most people who scan through sample web pages of online book retailers, such as the Kindle Store, then you indisputably said "yes." In this digital showground of online shopping, a book's cover is one of only a small number of features that you can utilize in making a choice of whether to purchase a certain book or whether to keep seeking for a better looking one.

You are no longer given the opportunity to physically judge possible purchases by the book's size, shape, or its placement on a bookstore shelf. To get book lovers to buy your eBook, you must captivate them by crafting an eBook cover that entices them to discover about your eBook.

Creating your eBook Cover

Designing an eBook cover yourself with Paint or Photoshop permits you the ability to fully customize a book cover to fit the precise manner you want your book embodied to your audience. Attempt taking advantage of free cover templates by searching the web for some sites that provide free eCover downloads. Play around with these techniques to get a basic sense of what pictures stand out, what looks good, and how to incorporate all your cover text into an eye-catching depiction. Take some time and try designing an eBook cover that you feel portrays the conception of your book to spectators.

If you have trouble creating your ideal cover, think about spending a little cash on using book cover creator software. These websites will usually offer you backgrounds, images, and lettering placement designs. If artistic design is just not for you, have somebody else create your eBook cover. This is as simple as outsourcing your cover design to private parties, such as individual designers, or professional parties, such as cover designing websites that have the necessary talents to syndicate all your ideas into a higher quality and professional-looking book cover.

When selecting how to design your eBook cover, please remember that you've worked hard at writing a quality eBook and that work deserves a quality package. Don't instantaneously settle for a cover design that you are not completely satisfied with just because it is free. Your eBook is an investment and spending a little bit of cash now can open the doors to making much more in the future.

Whatever your method for designing an eBook cover, it is essential that your entire book is showcased in an attention-grabbing package that clutches viewers' attention from numerous other eBooks and encourages them to indulge themselves in your particular work.

So now you have learned how to research, write, and format your digital books, it's time to get started. This idea with the many others in this book will need to be researched further before you venture out and try this as a money making avenue. Start with YouTube or UDEMY and get as much info as you can on making money online with e-books. The more information you have at the start the better you will do. This is not a get rich quick opportunity, but it is one that you can grow overtime to a substantial income.

Artists like musicians spend thousands of hours writing, singing and performing their work. But even after they are retired they still go on to earn huge income in royalties, so why not get into the royalty act as well with self-publishing.

Passive Income - Online Stores

It's the age of new technology where everything can be conveniently done with the use of a cellular phone, a laptop, or a computer, and now is the time to take advantage of this magnificent opportunity! Amazingly, you can now turn the hours you burn sitting on your computer chair while surfing the internet into something more productive!

Retail stores without an associated e-commerce website are quickly losing customers to the stress-free and convenient online shopping experience. This trend is convenient not only for the shoppers but for small business owners as well. Starting an online store and marketing it to a target market is much easier than purchasing retail space and advertisements. By following a few simple e-commerce tips when setting up the online store, small businesses are better equipped to compete with bigger retail stores.

So here's the rundown on how to make money online. Setting up online stores has been a very attractive work option for many already. If you have a skill for entrepreneurship and a product you could actually sell, and if you know your way around the internet well, then you might just find that an online store would be a great income generating activity online.

Of course, there are prerequisites before you can guarantee yourself a successful online business venture. Selling things online could prove to be very satisfying if it is done right. Many people actively buy products from websites and bidding sites because it saves time and effort on their part. Electronic paying options are bountiful, and shipping options are also flexible, thus making online shopping very pleasing to many. The sellers on eBay have already proven how effective online selling is. Perhaps, it is time you venture into it as well.

What to consider first before creating an online store:

1. Web site or a Seller account (Amazon, E-Bay, ETSY. Shopify etc.)?

First, you should consider which outlet you should create your store. Setting up your store's website requires a lot of effort and time. It also requires considerable knowledge of CSS and HTML. If you find this rather burdensome, you could just create a seller account, as it is much easier to create and you don't need to worry about generating traffic as there are already billions of buyers who already frequent these established platforms.

2. Which products to sell?

Before setting up your very own e-commerce store, you need to decide on what you are going to sell. Will the products be items that you have made yourself or products that you have purchased from wholesalers? What will make your online store or product different to what is already on offer by your competitors? Is there a high demand for your products?

It is easier to sell and promote a product if it's something you create or love. If you're into reading and book collecting, bookselling could be the thing for you. If you love fashion, then try putting up an online clothing store. It is easier to find a wholesale seller from which to get your products from if you are a secret lover of that product.

3. Product quality

The best approach to selling products online is to find loyal customers who will patronize your store, and this will only be done if you sell quality products. The quality inspection should be done first before you decide to put up a product for sale.

4. Time and Dedication

Online selling is much like a concrete store, for it to be successful; you will need patience, time and energy. If you dedicate ample time for it daily, you will be able to address some small glitches effectively. Your customers would also find you attentive and friendly.

When starting your online store, there are several platforms to choose from, and each of them comes with its pros and cons. Take BigCommerce for example; many people prefer it because of its ease of use and professional appearance. No matter which you decide to pick, here are a few steps that should not be overlooked.

Selecting a Domain Name:

Even though the domain name may seem minor, you should put a bit of thought into the word choice and make sure that it is relevant to your store and your target consumers. The domain name will affect your e-commerce website's ranking on search engines for certain keywords, driving more customers your way. For example, if you are selling watches, you might want to consider using the word "watch" in your domain name instead of something like "Bob's-Store."

Selecting a Payment Gateway:

While many platforms, such as BigCommerce, include their payment gateway, it's important to familiarize yourself with it and make sure that it is readily available for the customers. After all, this is the way you will get paid! If you don't already have a payment gateway set up, there are a few different options.

Typically, an e-commerce website either has a payment gateway and a merchant account. It is most efficient to have both, but either will do. Payment gateways are e-commerce services that authorize payments of the online store. PayPal is a commonly used example of this. A merchant account allows your store to accept Credit or Debit Card payments on your e-commerce website. Be sure to research the best options for your individual store.

Pricing Products:

When pricing the products in your online store, it's important to keep in mind the price of your competitors' products to make sure that you are not pricing products too high or too low. The other important thing to remember when pricing is to include the different options that can alter the price of a product (i.e. size, color, quantity, etc.). BigCommerce has very helpful tutorials that can walk you through the process of pricing various product options.

Selecting a Shipping Method:

An obvious difference between shopping online and in a store is the actual receipt of the product. If the goods are physical, you need to be sure and include a shipping method for your customers and make sure that the shipping costs are fair for both parties. There are three basic shipping strategies to use with your online store: free shipping, flat rate shipping, and variable rate shipping. It is best to use a combination of these three strategies. For example, offer free shipping (or a low flat rate) for any purchase over $100 and a variable rate for anything below that amount.

Setting Up Google Analytics:

Google Analytics is extremely useful in showing you pertinent information about visitors to your e-commerce website. Google Analytics is easy to use, and it tracks the visitors from search engines, online advertisements, e-mail campaigns, etc. It also gives you information about how often each person visits, and how well your different online ads are doing. The best part is that Google Analytics is completely free, so there is no reason not to use it!

Designing Your Online Store

Now that you've gotten started, one of the most important aspects of the website is the layout and design. Most platforms will offer you generic templates to start you off, but there are still some essential small design techniques that can make a big difference to the customer. You always want to be sure to keep the website clean, informative (without being too wordy) and unique.

Keeping it Clean:

Nobody likes a messy store where you have to dig through heaps of clothes to find the size you need. It's the same for online stores. If the customer has to put in more than a minimal amount of effort in looking for the product that they want, it isn't clean enough. To keep the e-commerce website clean, stick to the following three guidelines:

1) Maintain the product search bar where it is easy to locate on all pages of the site,

2) Maintain the amount of words and images on the homepage minimal so as not to overwhelm the customer (reducing the number of images will also lessen the amount of time it takes the page to load)

3) Use simple colors that do not clash -- an unappealing website will deter customers.

Including Just the Right Amount of Information:

The homepage should not be too wordy; you need to make sure that the customer has enough information to know the name of the store, the types of products sold, and a reason that this online store is superior to others that may seem similar.

Differentiating the Site:

Differentiating an e-commerce website can be done in a million different ways. It just takes going beyond the basic template and adding a touch of your store's unique personality to the design. This could be background music or a unique rotating banner. The aim to have an easy to use well laid out site that stands out.

Although many people, like me, do not possess the technical know-how to develop a unique and professional online store, Big Commerce design partners can help to modify the templates or even create entirely new models according to the individuals' preferences.

Once you have decided on your product and have started the process of setting up your e-commerce store then here are a few important things that you need to think about;

Who will take the photographs of the products that you will sell online? Will you write your copy or will you employ someone to do this for you? Don't just copy and paste what the manufacturer has given to you. There will be many other sellers that have done the same. Without a unique copy on your website store, the search engines won't pick up on your site, and it won't rank as high as you will want it to in the search engine results.

Where will you store the products that you will sell online? Do you have a garage or ample space in your home? How will you deliver the products ordered online? Will you charge a separate postage fee or will this be included in the price of the goods? What about orders which come from overseas? Will you charge a supplement for overseas delivery? How will you manage any returns or complaints? For all of these issues, you need to have clear and concise guidelines.

Once your e-commerce store is up and running, you need to get customers. To get visitors to your website, you will need to spend a considerable amount of time marketing your store and getting traffic. The first hurdle is to sell a product that people want to buy. Secondly, read up on what search engines want and set your site up in accordance with Search Engine Optimization guidelines.

Social media is an excellent technique to get traffic to your store, as is search engine optimization and offline promotions.

Once your e-commerce store is up and running, it is important to track and measure the performance of your store. This allows you to spot where there are any shortfalls and make any relevant changes /improvements. Google Analytics is one piece of software that lets you measure your advertising ROI (Return on investment) as well as tracking the source of your sales (social networking, affiliate networking or paid advertising).

Passive Income - Internet Marketing

If you already own a small business, and you think an online presence would be of great help, you are right. An Internet presence is a necessary evil, thanks to modern technology. However, that does not mean that it is not resource-draining. All this depends on your target audience and the type of your business.

If your primary approach is to build and maintain a website simply because everyone else is doing so, you are wrong. The main objective of online presence is to increase sales and boost your business growth and profitability.

Once you go ahead and develop a website, the next task is internet based marketing. It does not come free. You have to invest. There is a tremendous growth in the number of consumers who use Internet tools to search and purchase goods and services online.

What does that mean to you? Is there an increased opportunity? Yes, you are right. But it also means that there is robust competition. If your website does not announce its presence online, it will simply sit somewhere on a server gathering virtual dust. I hope you understand what I mean.

Let's now look at the most widely used tactics for free advertising and paid advertising on the internet.

Things to consider before starting

Even before starting, there are key questions you ought to ask yourself before starting any marketing efforts, whether on- or offline: "Who is my audience?" and "What are my objectives?"

Audience: The audience for most business marketing activities is obviously past, present, and future customers. However, as in traditional advertising and commercialization, it helps to narrow down who you are trying to reach, segmenting your market by age, geography, gender, interests, and occupation. Certain methods of Internet marketing, such as pay-per-click ads, allow you to target your customers based on this type of segmentation.

Objectives: We can assume that the overall goal of most marketing is to sell products and services, but you may have additional reasons for online marketing. These related objectives will hopefully end up driving increased sales, but they can be more long-term oriented than asking customers to buy right now. For example, your online marketing plan might include goals such as these:

   a) Support and increase the visibility of your company's brand.

b) Improve search engine rankings.

c) Offer reference information related to your business sector.

d) Increase the number of registered users or newsletter subscribers.

e) Drive traffic to your company website.

After defining your audience and marketing goals, you can begin to formulate your Internet marketing strategy and tactics. When getting into online marketing, it is important that you maintain brand consistency. Build on the reputation that you have already established. Your online presence should mirror that of your "brick and mortar" presence. Use the same logo and tagline so that people will understand that you are the same company. Having an online presence is a way to build on what you have already accomplished.

In the remainder of this topic, we'll look at the most common ways you can use the Internet to deliver your message and start increasing your sales.

Websites

We won't get into the vast topic of how to build and manage a website, but if you aim to use the techniques described below, it is essential to have one. Most of your marketing efforts will have a "call to action" that involves your audience visiting your website to research products or services, find contact information, sign up for a newsletter, or place an online order.

Whatever you are asking people to do in your online promotions, make sure the website allows them to complete that task easily. One other vital component of any business website is an analytics program (Google offers a fairly robust application free of charge) so you can track how well your marketing efforts are working and calculate the return on your advertising investment (ROI).

How can you develop an online presence at little or no cost? Several companies offer free site building tools and hosting services. If you go down this route, select a company that has a proven track record, so your hard work isn't wasted when the company goes out of business or suspends the service. Cheaper can sometimes mean less reliable.

A couple of reliable options are Google Sites and Yola. Budget for a decent domain name and hosting service as it will not only look professional but will pay dividends to your long-term efforts (for example, the domain name "www.mybusiness.com" looks more professional than "mybusiness.FreeCheapSkate.Hosting.com"). Another potential option, depending on your business and marketing goals, is to create a free blog (see below for more details). The most popular free blogging services as of this writing are WordPress and Blogger.

Email Newsletters

E-mail newsletters provide one of the most highly performing avenues for marketing. You can collect customer email addresses by asking visitors that come to your website to subscribe, by requesting e-mail addresses from anyone who visits your physical location, or by purchasing an e-mail list.

To generate a higher rate of readership, make sure the audience is narrowly targeted and has some vested interest in your product. By sending out your newsletter on a regular schedule (weekly, monthly, quarterly, etc.) you can counteract the transient and temporary nature of Internet users by continually reminding them of your company's existence. Affordable services like Constant Contact can be used to manage mailing lists, statistics, and opt-in/out functions.

A caveat: Sending commercial e-mail messages to people who have not agreed to receive your mailings can result in severe fines and penalties from the federal government per terms of the CAN-SPAM Act.

Newsletter content should appeal to your defined audiences, with industry- or product-related news and events, company-specific news and events, practical reference information, and interesting statistical and demographic information. The newsletter copy should publicize links to appropriate pages within your website.

You will need to maintain one or more separate lists for the purpose of sending targeted messages to particular audiences (see Other Announcements below). You might combine all your lists to send a monthly newsletter, and send other bulletins to the past or potential customers as appropriate.

Other Announcements

Other announcements are e-mailings that can consist of press releases, coupons, special notices, or anything you want to communicate individually to members of one or more e-mail lists.

Search Engine Optimization (SEO)

Search engine optimization means constructing a website that is easily crawled by search engine spiders, and it encompasses a variety of techniques designed to improve your site's (or page's) ranking in the search engine results page.

The goal is for your site to be found by searchers who are looking for sites related to a particular keyword or phrase, for example, "little red wagon" if you are in the business of selling toy wagons. SEO can be divided into one-page activities (e.g., amount of content, metadata, links, programming methods and structural issues) and off-page activities (most importantly, obtaining links from other websites to your site).

Pay-per-Click (PPC)

Pay-per-click advertising refers to text ads displayed on search engine result pages (versus "organic" results achieved by SEO) and other sites. In the case of Google AdWords and Microsoft's adCenter, you can open an account and specify the keyword(s) that, when searched for, will generate an ad that links to your website. You pay only when a searcher clicks an ad and is directed to your site.

A few of the benefits of PPC advertising are that you know exactly how many people view your ads, how many of those viewers click through to your website, and (if you are using a site analytics tool) what they do once they reach your site. You can also start and stop running ads at a moment's notice, experiment with any number of ads you like, and fund your campaign with as little as $10 to start.

Display Advertising

Display advertising, also called banner advertising, means purchasing ad space on another website and placing a text and graphic ad with a link to your site. This technique is more complicated and expensive than pay-per-click, but can be very powerful if the right message is shown to a tightly focused audience. To achieve optimal click-through rate (CTR), advertise on websites where you assume your target audience is visiting, rather than a general interest website. Most marketers don't purchase ad space directly from another website but use a banner ad network to place ads on appropriate websites automatically. A couple of the biggest names in display ad serving are DoubleClick and BurstMedia.

Social Media and Networking

Social networking is the latest buzz in the modern marketing arsenal. If you have any doubt about its impact, especially on the under-40 demographic, chances are you have been living under a rock. Small businesses with limited resources should weigh their time spent and the potential benefits carefully. It can also be difficult to measure the return on your investment for some of these tactics. Social Media is not a magic pill for success and in real business terms it doesn't always yield great ROI as people might think, so do your homework.

The general principle of "marketing" on social networking outlets is that people who have similar interests will virtually congregate around web content that discusses that interest. They may be interested in product information in the form of reviews or opinions, so hard sale approaches are mostly discouraged and unproductive.

Your goal is to become a trusted advisor; this may require revealing your identity and at least some part of your personality. If that premise makes you uncomfortable, you might still find social networking sites valuable for market research purposes. Find out what people are buying and why, then use that information to help shape your other marketing activities.

The following section describes the more popular social media outlets and sites but keeps your eyes open for new virtual spaces where you might get more attention by getting in on the ground floor.

YouTube, Facebook, and other platforms.

YouTube allows you to post videos on your "channel," a distinct Web page that can be customized and allows for posting links back to your website. A major positive aspect of this venue is that the number of views is published, and viewers can submit comments, so you know whether your videos are popular and why.

Facebook is considered the model for modern social networking sites. Facebook allows you (individual, corporate, non-profit, etc.) to create a page, attract "likes" and reviews, communicate with followers by posting status updates, photos and videos, and so on.

Although the previously named sites are the most popular in regards to visitors, there are a couple of business-oriented networking sites that may be more useful for making business connections. LinkedIn helps you develop a network of clients, service providers, and subject experts; find business opportunities and partners; post job openings; and more. More detailed advice on best practices for using LinkedIn can be found in many online articles and blogs.

Twitter

Think of Twitter as a mini-blog (see below) that allows you to broadcast messages of 140 characters or less. The messages appear to your "followers" on their phones or computers, as well as on Twitter.com. The biggest challenges are to gain a useful number of followers and to think of something engaging when writing to them. If you are a speaker, writer, or performer Twitter can be used to let your fans know what you're doing and when. If you have a retail store, you might let your followers know that you're offering a discounted item or running a special sale. You should post a Twitter sign-up link on your website, and within your signature line in outgoing e-mail messages. You can also gain followers by following people who work in or comment in your industry, as some Twitter users will follow those who follow them.

Blogs

The word blog originally came from the term "Web log." There's no real standard for what a blog is, but most commonly authors use them to comment on (and link to) other online news items, websites, or other Internet content. For the most part, direct selling on a blog is frowned upon and is probably a recipe for driving away potential readers. What do you write about, then?

Well, if you run an Internet marketing firm you write about trends in Web marketing, what the search engines are up to, tips for do-it-yourselfers, or what you thought of the latest Hollywood blockbuster. Seriously, read some blogs and you will find all sorts of opinion mixed in with professional advice and commentary. The goal of your blog, however, should most likely be to establish yourself as an expert and trusted advisor in your chosen field.

You might also pursue getting your products, services, or website mentioned in related blogs by other industry experts. When a high-visibility blogger mentions a website on his or her blog, the site is exposed to a potential audience of new viewers. Often, blog postings are simply press releases that are picked up by sites that discuss topics related to a particular product or industry. More opportunities (and traffic) in this arena can be realized by developing relationships with individual bloggers.

Additional Tips:

Others write post articles, just be sure to provide a link to the original article and give credit to the authors. You can then offer your commentary on the topic of the article or find a way to relate the information to local trends or challenges.

Ask colleagues to be "guest bloggers" by writing articles for you to post, again giving them credit and adding their byline and a link to their website. Using links is a good way to drive additional traffic to their sites, so it's a good trade-off for both parties.

Forums & Discussion Groups

A forum (also known as a discussion group, message board or bulletin board) is a component of a website where users can ask questions, offer advice, or share experiences with others about a certain topic or topics. Nearly every hobby on earth has some popular forums wherein members provide their thoughts and feelings on all aspects of their favorite pastime. Contributing a comment (with a link to your website) in discussion groups related to your products or services can create a small surge or spike in traffic, but has a long-lasting effect. Target forums on high-traffic sites that have 1,000+ users but still reply to topics with larger numbers of views (relative to other posted topics) to maximize effectiveness.

You can easily build your bulletin board/forum component on your site with free or low-cost software. User forums have the potential to significantly increase the "stickiness" of a site, given a critical mass of traffic required to generate new discussions and keep participants interested in returning.

You can start by "seeding" topics on your own, but there won't be any results until traffic is directed to the forums. The conundrum for small businesses may be the time required to moderate a forum once it becomes successful. One solution is to seek out a volunteer moderator who exhibits a keen interest in your field.

Article Placement / E-Zines

Another avenue for generating incoming links and traffic to your site is the free article market. Article submission (or e-zine) websites allow you to publish articles on a variety of topics.

Depending on terms of use, these articles may be used as content on other websites, or collected on the sites of the original submission. The main objective of most article contributors is to increase their search engine rankings with the placement of back links on other reputable sites. Providing reliable and accurate reference information is secondary, and the traffic potential from article readers is questionable.

Obtaining links from article submission sites isn't likely to improve your site's search engine rankings much. However, existing content from a print newsletter or other written material can be re-purposed with a relatively small time investment.

Be aware that creating articles from your website's content verbatim may cause search engines to penalize your site, as the search engines take a dim view of text that is republished multiple times ("duplicate content" in search engine optimization terms). Submitting articles to sites with the most traffic will give your site the best chance to be discovered by new readers.

Caveat: Once an article is submitted, you have little or no control over who uses your content and for what purpose, depending on the copyright policies of the site on which the article is posted.

Other Internet Marketing Outlets

Wikipedia

Wikipedia is, essentially, an online encyclopedia. The unique aspect of Wikipedia is that users generate the content, though volunteer editors must approve content. Traffic will grow if and when others link to the entry. If you add content, your time commitment will be relatively minor, and the benefits might include improved search engine ranking and a slight increase in traffic to your site.

As with other forms of Internet communication, a Wikipedia entry that is a commercial for a product, service, or company will not be viewed positively and is unlikely to be approved by editors.

Directories

Online directories allow Internet users to browse through categories of topics to find websites related to an individual subject. There are lists for businesses, blogs, websites in general, and more. Many directories are free, and some only list you if you pay. The mother of free directories is the Open Directory Project, and by all accounts, the best-paid directory for business is the Yahoo! Directory ($299 annually). Be aware that you might wait a long time for some of the free directories to list your site, as they may rely on volunteer screeners. Directories not only allow consumers to find you in their listings, but they also help get your site indexed in the major search engines. If you submit your site to a directory, make sure to read the submission guidelines and follow them exactly.

Final Thoughts

People don't become rich or poor by chance. Wealth is not created by positive thinking. But positive thinking does precede wealth. What sets apart wealthy people from those who struggle is not just thoughts but most importantly the actions and responsibilities rich people take in securing their future. Those who passed through the educational system have been taught to rely on their jobs as the principle means of wealth creation followed by their homes. But the fact is this elaborate Ponzi scheme is slowly becoming unravelled and is no longer sustainable as many developed countries especially the USA and the UK have trillion dollars of debt that the future generations will struggle to pay off.

This book is not about affluence but about little simple ideas anyone can use to become wealthy. You may not be familiar with all the concepts and may feel a little lost in some places, but what you must do from that point is take your time and delve into further research.

Many of the individual topics mentioned here are individual books in their own write so, my aim was to simply introduce some of you into ways of making money you are not familiar with.

It is clear that the process of becoming rich starts from the understanding of the principles of personal finance. These include managing your income, managing your expenses and debts, and the ability to save and invest.

While those who end up rich strive to earn more and save a substantial portion of their income, the folk that end up poor by the time of retirement are never worried about their earnings. However, the real difference comes where the "poor" group spends all their income on non-essentials and get into debt just to finance their luxury life while the "wealthy" concentrate on saving and investing to guarantee future streams of cash flows.

A lot can be said, and much has been mentioned, but unless you put some of what you have learned so far into practice, all you have read so far remains theory.

Wealth is a choice that you can make. In this book we looked at some of the traditional ways to make more money as well as some of the techniques you can learn to make money on the internet.

Don't languish in poverty when this book breaks down complex topics like real estate investment, stocks, bonds and mutual funds and the internet and passive income alternatives, that you can start today and increase your income. I have heard many say they can't afford to invest yet spend hundreds of dollars financing a luxury car each month.

I hope this book has encouraged you to make a paradigm shift in your thinking and will help you re-direct your surplus income into investments and not vain frivolous spending.

It is highly critical in today's society, given the instability of the economy, for people to invest their money wisely. Many people might rationalize that investing is rather complicated and intricate, but the reality is, one needs to put strategies in place to survive. One simply needs to invest their money. Invest in what you might ask? All these questions have been answered.

Finally, if you enjoyed this book, please take some time to share your thoughts and post a review on Amazon. It would be greatly appreciated.

Thank you and let's stay connected

Thanks for reading my book. I would like to send you free copies of my books and others from my publisher from time to time.

Please click on the image to register and receive free content and a chance to will a great prize.

Other stuff

Follow on social media

Printed in Great Britain
by Amazon